AUTHORITY
ENCOUNTER

EMBRACING GOD'S MISSION FOR YOU

CHUCK DAVIS

FOREWORD BY CHARLES KRAFT

Library of Congress Cataloging-in-Publication Data is on file

For inquiries about volume orders, please contact:

Beaufort Books
27 West 20th Street, Suite 1102
New York, NY 10011
sales@beaufortbooks.com

Published in the United States by Beaufort Books
www.beaufortbooks.com

Distributed by Midpoint Trade Books
www.midpointtrade.com

Printed in the United States of America

Interior design by Thunder Mountain Design
Cover Design by Scott Sawala

To

Ingrid, my best friend, wife, and

partner in spiritual warfare,

and

Linnea, Christian, and Jordan,

my three adult children who

valiantly walked with us into

challenging places for the sake

of the kingdom.

Your partnership has made it easy

for me to lead us under the

Lordship of Jesus Christ.

Table of Contents

Foreword

Satan is scared to death that we'll find out who we are and start behaving like we should. He can't be happy about this book or the very few others that deal with our authority as Christ followers. Chuck Davis has approached his subject as both a student and a practitioner in discovering what a Christian's authority is all about and, in a very readable style, both informed and challenged us to wake up to the privilege and responsibility that is ours to live and minister in Jesus's authority. As he points out, this authority is not simply a spiritual gift that only a few are given but a part of the equipping Jesus gives to all believers. Thank you, Chuck, and with you, I bless all who read this book with the commitment to practice the authority Jesus has given them.

Charles Kraft
January 2013

Preface

Vehicles arrive at the crossroads anxious to continue through the intersection. A twenty-ton truck bounces down the hill in the direction of an intersection. A traffic officer standing in the middle of the converging vehicles raises his white-gloved hand: "Stop." The truck skids to a halt. Why? The truck is clearly more powerful than the officer. In one word—**authority!** It is not the physical power of the officer that changes the circumstance. It is the authority of the badge that he wears and the government sovereignty that ensures the authority behind the badge.

Traffic officers are not common in all areas of the world, but in my town in the suburbs of metro New York, they still govern the main avenue. When I first moved to this town, I was unaware of how much invested authority they held, even for pedestrians. I once stepped into the crosswalk without the officer's go-ahead and was met with a bellowing reprimand. I am since very cautious in my movements—the authority lines are now clear to me.

I also lived in a capital city in West Africa, where traffic officers were positioned on most major corners. I saw a similar scenario played out daily: a massive truck bearing down on the intersection. The police officer would enter the intersection with arms waving and whistles blowing but sometimes with a different outcome. The truck would barrel through without concern. Why? The truck driver was operating from the guiding principle that **power** was the final word because the **authority** behind the police officer was suspect. The government could not ensure the authority behind the badge.

I find that the natural and social world mimics or illustrates the spiritual world. Jesus clearly made the connection between natural and spiritual. His teaching is rather simple in its use of metaphor and social nuance, but it is deep in revealed spiritual principle. I have come to realize that one of the key aspects of the journey of being a Christ follower is this notion of **authority**. We live in a world that is rooted in power. We are daily challenged by powers that seek to interrupt or even trample our success in the journey. If we try to win by out-powering the opposition, we will always face an uncertain future and a lack of peaceful confidence such as that rooted in Christ; we win when we are more powerful but lose when we are less powerful. However, if we embrace the principle that God wants us to live out of His delegated **authority**—an authority recovered by Jesus and passed on to us—we will live with a greater sense of God's security in the mysteries of life. This is the Authority of the Believer!

My premise   Authority always trumps power in the
                  spiritual world.

My conviction   A biblically rooted understanding of
                  authority is one of the most important
                  aspects of the Christ-life.

My practice   Living in spiritual authority, I have
                  experienced the delight of watching
                  God's kingdom manifest in the face of
                  powerful opposition.

My vision   Invite every Christ follower to
                  embrace this provision from God.

Introduction

A man battles his fleshly, natural tendencies. He feels caught in the roaring middle of Paul's "I do what I don't want to do" (Roman 7). He tries white-knuckling it, placing all of his strength into the battle against his desires but without success. Behavioral modification is not the answer. He tries counseling and accountability groups. These help but are not completely effective. He approaches his spiritual leaders for a fresh impartation of the Holy Spirit. This renews his resolve but does not lead to long-term change. Then he hears about his position in Christ and the resulting authority that he carries. When the urges come, he stands in authority and places the temptation squarely underneath his feet. He rejoices to find himself overcoming!

A woman feels a strong presence come over her while sleeping at night. It sits on her chest and chokes her. She cannot speak, even to get out one word: "Jesus." It happens every time she makes a decision for renewed commitment to serve God or at transitional points in her life. Each time she feels paralyzed. She is afraid to share her experience with others because a naturalistic worldview has pushed her to bury spiritual realities under a more "reasonable" explanation. If she told others, people would think her crazy or attribute a psychological reason for the dreams. Then she learns about the authority that she has been given through her relationship with Christ. The next time the attack comes, she does not speak with her own power but with her invested authority. The evil presence flees!

A young couple is perplexed with the nightmares that wake up their two-year-old son every night. The son wakes up screaming in terror and wet with sweat, and will not return to sleep. This repeats for months. They pray, get counsel, try to comfort, everything they can imagine to help their son and bring sanity back to the household. They hear a teaching about their position in Christ, especially their invested authority as gatekeepers for their family. Without the little boy's knowledge, they anoint his room with oil and take on their authority. Their son sleeps straight through the night, and peace is the new pattern of the household!

I have tested the principles of spiritual authority in multiple roles and places around the world as a follower of Christ. Through my preaching and teaching ministry I have also observed others taking hold of these principles and the resulting radical changes in their lives. The stories above are true and repeated multiple times in my experience. I want you to see what is at stake. The promise of the Scriptures is that we would be overcomers in Christ. Yet many times we feel far from that reality. At times our apparent failures are because we have not appropriated our authority in Christ.

With this introduction, I must tell you of some of my underlying presuppositions so that you read me in context. First, God is primarily interested in a relationship with us, not performance from us. God loves you just the way you are. You cannot do anything to add to that love nor take away from that love. But it goes one step further. God loves you so much that He will not leave you in the condition that you find yourself. His design is that from within that loving relationship you would cooperate with Him to become more like Jesus (to know Christ) and to be a full partner in His kingdom project to restore others to that relationship (to make Christ known). And God is serious about the full partnership piece: He likes to delegate responsibility and authority to accomplish the task. But the goal is never about performance!

Second, one of the most consistent backdrops to the biblical narrative is spiritual warfare. Two kingdoms are at battle—the kingdom of darkness versus the kingdom of light—both powerful. From the first pages of the Bible to the last, this theme is the context for the interactions between God and people, people and people, people and themselves, people and the worldly systems around them, and people and the spirit world. The kingdom of darkness, though powerful, is an inferior kingdom. The kingdom of light is superior but still must step up to reclaim what was stolen from it. The kingdom of light does have an advantage—a restored and appropriated authority through Jesus Christ!

Third, the authority of the believer is not a gimmick or a magic wand against trouble in our lives. Authority flows from our relationship and our position in Christ. If I take the apostle Paul seriously, knowing Christ involves celebrating in the victory of his present risen-ness and sometimes sharing in his suffering, even unto death (Philippians 3). Because God is more interested in who I am becoming than in my comfort level, sometimes becoming like Jesus and helping others experience him in the same way will place me in the middle of suffering, hardship, and trouble. Mysteriously, sometimes suffering is part of God's plan to shape us and use us to help others in this world that is broken. Thus I do not embrace a theology that states that a Christ follower operating with authority will never face challenging circumstances. In fact, the Bible suggests just the opposite. I instead want to arm us with authority to stand against the opposition and brokenness that are not part of God's design to bring a greater good in and through our lives.

In this book, I will unfold the principles of the authority of the believer, beginning with descriptions of this theological concept as depicted in the word of God. Chapter one will describe how humans forfeited their authority. Chapter two will trace the recovery of authority by Jesus Christ. Chapter three will highlight how Jesus has restored this once-forfeited authority to his followers.

After setting the biblical–theological foundation of

spiritual authority, I will offer some contemporary principles and guidelines for the use of our authority. Chapter Four will offer some examples of how spiritual authority becomes useful in our daily lives. Chapter Five will offer some practical guidelines for the proper use of authority. Chapter Six will suggest an action plan to move forward.

My purpose is to show how the notions of spiritual authority flow deeply from God's word and how spiritual authority, once understood, becomes a vital component to living out our Christian faith as overcomers. An understanding and appropriation of spiritual authority has profoundly impacted my life and the lives of others that I have had the privilege of leading to a similar understanding. Much is at stake in the believer's spiritual authority.

CHAPTER ONE

Authority Forfeited

The creation accounts of Genesis 1–3 have fallen into controversy in recent years. So much discussion has been invested in the *how* and the *timing* of the events of Creation that we have missed the most important element of God's revelation in these texts. It is not so much a scientific manifesto as it is a theological description that explains the purposefulness of Creation, God's hand and original design in Creation, and why creation feels out of balance so much of the time. These narratives also introduce the notion of authority.

When God created Adam and Eve (humanity), He placed them in a position of authority over the rest of creation. This authority is described in the notions of **ruling** and **subduing**:

Then God said, "Let us make man in our image, in our likeness, and let them **rule** over . . .

So God created man in his own image . . . male and female he created them . . .

> God blessed them and said to them, "Be fruitful
> and increase in number; fill the earth and **subdue**
> it. **Rule** over . . .
>
> (Selections from Genesis 1:26–28)

This ruling and subduing is rooted in a deep sense of stewardship rather than exploitation or abuse. Being created in the image of God means that we were designed to rule in the same manner as Him—which is always beneficial for *those being ruled over*—not in manipulation or abusive control. This aspect of constructive—not destructive—subjugation is seen in the use of two Hebrew verbs in Genesis 2:15, where humans are given the assignment to care for the garden. The first verb is *abad*, which can be translated as "work," "nurture," "sustain," or "husband"; the second is *shamar*, which implies "safeguard," "preserve," "care for," or "protect." These verbs capture the idea of humans working alongside God in nurturing the flourishing of the world, with an attitude of cherishing and stewardship. Our stewardship role is a continual theme throughout the Scriptures.

This assignment to exercise authority over the rest of creation is also emphasized in the action of naming depicted in the Genesis 2 Creation narrative.

> Now the Lord God had formed out of the ground
> all the beasts of the field and all the birds of the air.

He brought them to the man to see what he would
name them; and what the man called each living
creature, that was its name.

(Genesis 2:19)

In the biblical worldview, naming is more than assigning
a label to an object. The act of naming something implies
having authority over that object. God could easily have
given names to that which He declared as good, but He
chose to give that authority to humans. It is important to
see this delegation of rulership as creative design.

The Psalmist recounts this purposefulness with a sense
of awe that leads to celebration of the name of the Lord:

When I consider your heavens,
the work of your fingers,
the moon and the stars,
which you have set in place,
what is man that you are mindful of him,
the son of man that you care for him?
You made him a little lower than heavenly beings
and crowned him with glory and honor.

You made him ruler over the works of your hands;
you put everything under his feet:
all flocks and herds, and beasts of the air,
and the fish of the sea, all that swim the paths of

the seas.
O Lord, our Lord, how majestic is your name in all
the earth!

(Psalm 8:3–9)

Some scholars point to the suggestion of Messianic antici-
pation in this psalm. The phrase "you put everything under his feet" will come up later in this book's description of
the positioning of Christ's authority in the Christ-event, as
well as in the positioning of the Christ follower. However,
the Psalmist is looking back to Creation as well. This psalm
makes it clear that humans have a unique place in the creative order. That position comes with the vocation of rulership. This authority is based on notions of stewardship
rather than ownership; thus we are called to rule in light of
God's design and manner.

Forfeited Privilege and Complicated Stewardship

When Adam and Eve chose to obey Satan instead of
God, they to some degree gave Satan legal right to rule on
the earth. It is not my purpose to go into detail regarding
the narrative of the Fall (Genesis 3). I will simply note that
the order God created out of chaos was turned back to chaos through a usurped authority structure. The serpent in
the narrative (Satan and the kingdom of darkness) tempts
Adam and Eve (humanity) to operate in a system other

than the original design. This rebellion against the original way is seen in the wording of the temptation: "Did God really say…?" (Genesis 3:1).

The results are simple: a broken relationship expressed in shame and hiding (3:8), a life of struggle rooted in power domination versus spiritual authority (3:16), and work experienced as cursed toil rather than stewardship (3:17–19). Through the introduction of, and the obedience to, another ruler, the natural cooperation with God in exercising His authority became an unnatural struggle.

Beyond the enmity that was introduced into the system, a new authority structure was established. Satan was given a new level of authority in the transaction. The legal right and transfer of rulership at this event are assumed in several titles that are given for Satan in the Bible. Satan became

"the prince of this world" (John 12:31, 14:30, 16:11),
"prince of the power of the air" (Ephesians 2:2), and
"god of this age" (2 Corinthians 4:4).

The biblical narrative states directly, "The whole world is under the control of the evil one" (1 John 5:19). The word translated as "world" in this instance is *cosmos* (χοσμοσ) and has three basic meanings when used in the New Testament, depending on the context:

(1) the earth or creation (see John 17:24),
(2) people in the world (see John 3:16), or
(3) the systems of this world that oppose God's
    design (see Ephesians 2:1–3).

In the context of 1 John 5:19, the third meaning makes the most sense because what Satan controls and rules are the worldly systems that are in opposition to the actions of the children of God. He does not have control of the whole earth or of all people. The key is the issue of rulership and control. Satan used this stolen authority in the temptation of Jesus in Luke 4. He showed Jesus the kingdoms of the world (definition (3): systems) and declared, "I will give you all their authority . . . for it has been given to me, and I can give it to anyone I want to" (4:6). This was not false bravado. Interpreters who make this claim fail to see that Satan's authority was not given by God but by humans.

This shifting of legal right turns our stewardship into conflict and power. We find ourselves fighting to take back what was rightfully ours at Creation. The apostle Paul described his own calling in Acts 26:18:

To open their eyes and turn them from darkness to light, and from the power of Satan to God, so that they might receive the forgiveness of sins and a place among those who are sanctified by faith in [Jesus].

The links between darkness and the power of Satan are obvious. That power is substantial and it is invested with a level of authority that was forfeited by humans at the Fall.

An important distinction is that Satan stole our (humans') authority, not God's authority. All authority ultimately flows from God's throne, but the devil does not usurp God's authority; he usurps our authority as stewards of creation. We do not believe in a dualism, in two separate but equal powers, which suggests that Satan is toe-to-toe with God. Satan is a fallen angel, created by God and in rebellion against God. The cosmic battle between his kingdom and God's kingdom is intense. Mysteriously, God allows Satan's stolen authority to be used to oppose God's good creative purpose. The Bible repeatedly reminds us that the Christ follower operates in the midst of this conflict. The prize or plunder in the battle between the kingdom of darkness and the kingdom of light is earthly territory and, more importantly, the people who bear God's image. God wants and invites us to be part of the restoration process— to re-exercise authority and to take back what rightfully was created to reflect God's glory (light) and not the fallen state (darkness).

Anti-Authority Bias in America and Other Cultural Contexts

Americans have a deep-seated bias against authority. We assume that hierarchy and notions of authority that come from hierarchy are bad. This deep response is rooted in our history, culture, and contemporary social structure. Most recently, pop culture and trends of authority abuse have invigorated this backlash against authority.

Historically, our nation was founded by rebellion. Early settlers left oppressive political and religious authorities in Europe to espouse what was declared as in "liberty and freedom for all." At the very core of this emigration was a statement against hierarchical authority. This stand against authority is necessary at times. Jesus and Martin Luther King, Jr. both stood against the religious and political authorities of their day to bring about a better good. Both did this in the way of the kingdom of God (see Matthew 5–7). Nevertheless, any action, even if done for the right reasons, still has the potential to swing too far and have negative consequences.

One of the core cultural and social values from the beginning of American history is the dignity of all human beings. This is expressed in the ideal of egalitarian relationships and in individualism. Over the years the idea of individualism has shifted from individual worth to individual autonomy. The individualism of the American fathers was rooted in community accountability. The individual had worth and autonomy, with a goal to use that position for the greater good of the community. Over time, this independence became an over-expressed individualism and a suspicion of hierarchy and positions of authority.

The pop-culture response came in an antiauthoritarian movement that was a natural outcome of the misuse of power by authorities in America. In the late 1950s and 1960s, with the help of the media, the misuse of political, religious, and business authority was exposed. At the same time, postmodernism legitimized the questioning of what we always assumed to be true. This questioning was good and necessary. But this questioning, originally done for the right reasons, has swung even further and has become a spirit of cynicism toward any notion of authority or benefit of hierarchical order. This antiauthoritarian sentiment has become a larger part of our underlying values than we realize.

These deep-rooted reflexes in us are important to recognize as they can be stumbling blocks to living out a structure of authority restored by adherence to biblical principles. Authority is not bad, but the misuse of authority is. One step of the process of restoring the original structure of authority is for us to use authority properly—in the Jesus Way. (Chapter 5 will offer practical guidelines for using authority in the way of God's kingdom.)

Balanced Perspective on Satan and
the Kingdom of Darkness

It is important at this point in the discussion to be sure that we have a clear understanding of the nature of Satan and his work. C.S. Lewis, in his classic work *The Screwtape Letters*, warns of two dangers that rest on opposite sides of a continuum: to overestimate and, equally, to underestimate the power of Satan and the kingdom of darkness. To overestimate Satan is to live in unwarranted fear, which takes us away from our primary focus on Jesus. To underestimate Satan is to live in denial of danger, which leaves us victim to attacks that could otherwise be easily resisted, and which surrenders our invitation from God to be proactive overcomers.

Satan's authority and his ability to act are limited. He is clearly under the authority of God. This principle is stated in the story of Job, where Satan must have permission from God to oppose Job (Job 1:6–12, 2:6). This narrative is difficult to comprehend fully. The obvious question is, why does God grant that permission? A number of my students have posed the question in another way: "Why doesn't God just stamp Satan out?" The simplest answer is that God's allowance for Satan is a mystery, and I am not sure that human reason will be able to come up with a more satisfying answer. Many of life's big questions remain unanswerable, and this is captured in the ongoing dialogue of God and

Job: "Where were you when I laid the earth's foundations? Tell me if you understand" (Job 38:4). These unanswerable questions are not intended to create despair. They offer instead the opportunity to refocus. Are further questions or insights perhaps hidden underneath? Whatever the reason, God has chosen to leave them unanswered, and I have to believe that is for our good.

One insight for me is that God's sovereignty—the umbrella authority—somehow operates without violating the other forms of authority that He has freely passed on to us. To describe it another way, God constantly orchestrates a great symphony, but the musicians have the responsibility to play their individual parts. If God were to stomp on Satan, it would be the same as stomping on our free will—a violation of God's character, which is of invitation and not of control.

Again the freedom God gives Satan is mysterious because Satan directly opposes the glory of God, which seems like a legitimate thing for God to obliterate. In doing so, however, God guarantees the larger composition—that which was created as good will ultimately be restored—but He chooses to allow His creation to partner in the process, for better or for worse.

The limited authority of Satan is also related to its stolen nature. Satan is a thief, a parasite. He is not a creator but a counterfeiter. His authority depends on the cooperation of human beings. Scripture gives a clear analogy of how our refusal to cooperate impacts his ability to exercise authority. "Do not give the devil a foothold" (Ephesians 4:27). "Resist the devil and he will flee from you" (James 4:7). Satan works through strongholds that he has gained in territory, culture, society, and our flesh. Charles Kraft uses the analogy of garbage to refer to a place of stronghold, and the analogy of rats to refer to the kingdom of darkness (*Deep Wounds Deep Healing*). Rats are drawn to garbage, he says. If you want to rid a city block of rats, you will be more successful cleaning up the garbage than chasing every rat. Satan's ability to work is equal to the amount of garbage that we leave in our lives.

Sin creates garbage. This garbage can be places of active rebellion in our lives against God's design. Deuteronomy 28 chronicles two ways in life—the way of blessing and the way of curse—either of which we have free will to select. Sadly, the garbage can also be the wounds from evil done to us or lived out in the community around us.

These damaged places attract the kingdom of darkness. They need healing to be transformed from places of hurt to places of brokenness. The physical counterpart is the transformation of wound to scar. The scar does not hold physical pain but is a reminder of the original wound and the subsequent healing. Spiritually, God uses brokenness as a testimony to His healing transformation. When we do not seek healing, the garbage continues to collect in our wounds, in the footholds carved out by the enemy of our soul, and the pile becomes so large that we may no longer see beyond the pain. The pain becomes part of our identity and is expressed outwardly in our attitudes and actions. At this point, Satan's foothold becomes a stronghold, and the sense of bondage becomes more debilitating. Nigel Wright says in *The Satan Syndrome*, "The vitality of the devil is parasitic and his strength drawn from humanity...the power the devil has in himself is far less than we might imagine and far more dependent on that which mankind gives him."

While I want us to understand the limited authority of Satan, at the same time I do not want us to miss the exhaustive, vile, and dangerous nature of Satan's work and the kingdom of darkness. Both hiding our heads in the sand and having a premature sense of triumph will keep us from proactively taking back our delegated authority to partner with God in His restoration project. There are clear biblical examples of Satan hindering the work of God's servants. In Daniel 10, demonic princes block angelic beings in their movements and travel. The account implies a link between the movements of heavenly spirits and the earthly prayer and fasting of Daniel. Jesus himself was opposed by Satan, under the guidance of the Holy Spirit (Matthew 4:1–11). The apostle Paul, too, says, "For we wanted to come to you . . . again and again—but Satan stopped us" (1 Thessalonians 2:18). At other times Paul attributes the direction and movements of his ministry to the guidance of the Holy Spirit. We understand from these references that he sees a struggle between kingdoms for the advance of the work of Christ. The calling of Paul puts him in the midst of this struggle "to turn them from darkness to light, and from the power of Satan to God" (Acts 26:18).

Our general calling is not different from Paul's. To be in a relationship with God through Christ is to operate with His desires. Peter reminds us that God "is patient with [us], not wanting anyone to perish, but everyone to come to repentance" (2 Peter 3:9). So we join Paul as ministers of reconciliation, "as though God were making his appeal through us" (2 Corinthians 5:20). When we consider our calling in light of Jesus's interpretation of the Parable of the Sower, we are reminded that we have a personalized force working against us. As Jesus interprets the parable for His disciples, He gives several reasons why God's word is not fruitful in every person who receives it, including that Satan comes and takes away the word (Mark 4:1–20). Thus the opposition of Satan is very real and determinedly obstructs the progress of God's restoration project.

In the end, what we do know is that even these setbacks and struggles somehow fall under God's larger plan and authority. It calls us to a place of trust and not fear. Joseph of the Old Testament declares to his brothers, "You intended harm to me, but God intended it for good to accomplish what is now being done, the saving of many lives" (Genesis 50:20). I gain a better perspective from these words. But my trust is not a passive one. God has done something in the life of Jesus that restores the authority forfeited in the Creation narrative. In fact, He empowers us with a renewed claim to our received authority and to return to our calling by God to rule. We move on to the Christ-event and the reclaiming of our authority through Jesus.

Unquestioned Authority Bias in Shame-Based Cultures

I n the same manner that Americans have blind spots in relation to authority, other cultures have theirs. In some shame-based cultures, the societal rules are so established in hierarchy that questioning authority is forbidden. Any structure that does not permit critique is ripe for the abuse of authority. This is especially true of political and religious institutions, which carry an assumed authorization and legitimization of a higher order.

In the case of forced authority that is not for the good of the group, people will comply as long as they are led to believe that they are better off subjugated, and as long as enough people experience social mobility to keep the dream of advancement alive. But since all authority ultimately comes from God, misuse through force by a human authority will lead to that authority's undoing. In the state, it raises an outcry that leads to a coup d'état and often a repeating cycle of tyranny. New powers must choose whether to operate through their freshly wielded power or through systems of righteous authority.

In the context of religion, misuse of authority connected with disempowerment leads to frustration and often a wandering from the faith. I have observed this dynamic in first- and second-generation Asian immigrant groups in the

New York metropolitan area. The hierarchical social structure of Asian cultures causes first-generation leaders to hold absolute authority. This authority is not passed on to younger leaders. The next generation, raised in the American cultural context, becomes frustrated and desires a level of trust and empowerment that invites them to take on delegated authority. This generation either remains an untapped spiritual resource or they simply walk away from the faith. Their experience of faith has been one of a system of control rather than as a journey in a relationship with God and others.

This defensive clinging to authority is utterly opposite to God's own pattern. At Creation, He willingly delegated authority. We will see in the next chapter that Jesus begins the process of passing on authority early in his ministry. The challenge for these cultural and social structures will be a reclaimed biblical authority that bears the marks of the Servant Leader. This authority may be exercised in strong hierarchical structures or in a more flattened, egalitarian approach. Both have the potential to reclaim authority in a biblically consistent manner.

CHAPTER TWO

The Christ Event and Authority

fter examining the impact of the Fall and the result of forfeited authority, we would be despondent if not for the Christ-event. The Christ-event is everything surrounding the incarnation of the Son, the second person of the Trinity, the God-man Jesus—his life, death, resurrection, ascension, and second coming. As we observe the successive stages of the Christ-event, we see that authority is restored by degrees of positioning of Jesus Christ in authority and that God's order is progressively restored in the new creation. The kingdom of the "now but not yet" advances. We must begin with the purpose for Jesus's first coming.

Jesus and the Kingdom

Why did Jesus come? Theologically we know that the deep-rooted answer to this question is redemption. What was lost after Creation—in the Fall—is realigned at Jesus's incarnation, crucifixion, and resurrection. God is restoring creation, and Jesus is the centerpiece of that restoration program. Arthur Glasser, in his book *Announcing the kingdom,* illustrates how this restoration is structured in Scripture:

GENESIS	REVELATION
Paradise lost	Paradise regained
Creation of heaven and earth	A new heaven and earth
The curse enters (sin, sorrow, suffering, death)	No more curse
Tree of Life guarded	Tree of Life restored
Communion destroyed	Communion restored
Work cursed	Work blessed
People out of harmony with nature	People at peace with nature

We can see this unfolding through Jesus in the announcement of the kingdom of God—God's rule—and in one very direct statement from the 1st Epistle of John that interprets the reason for Jesus's coming.

First, to announce the kingdom of God. Jesus declared, "I must preach the good news of the kingdom of God, because that is **why I was sent**" (Luke 4:43). The central theme to Jesus's teaching was the coming of the kingdom of God. The kingdom is referenced over ninety times in the gospels alone. John the Baptist prepared those who would receive Jesus with the same message: "The time has come, the kingdom of God is near" (Mark 1:15). Jesus affirmed John the Baptist's message (Luke 16:16), and he proclaimed the good news of the kingdom (Luke 8:1). Jesus moved beyond proclaiming the kingdom of God, however, to demonstrating that it was already here.

Luke 4:14–21 is viewed as Jesus's "coming out" or statement of purpose in the gospels. In this account, Jesus was in the synagogue in his hometown of Nazareth and was called upon to read the Scripture for the day, a passage from Isaiah 61, from the sacred scroll. The passage describes various manifestations of the presence of God's kingdom including anointing by the Holy Spirit, preaching good news, release of the oppressed, healing, and God's favor. Jesus declared, "Today, this Scripture is fulfilled in your hearing" (4:21). He then proceeded to initiate a ministry that demonstrated the coming of the kingdom with a threefold plan of action: preaching or announcing the kingdom, healing, and casting out demons. He said, "If I drive out demons by the finger of God, then the kingdom of God has come" (Luke 10:20). In fact, when John the Baptist from his prison cell sent a delegation as reassurance that he had not been mistaken about Jesus's identity, Jesus told the messengers to respond with what they had seen and heard—the preaching of the good news and its demonstration through healing (Matthew 11:1–5).

When Jesus passed on this calling to his followers, they were commissioned with the same action plan:

When Jesus had called the Twelve together, he

gave them power and authority to drive out all demons and to cure diseases, and he sent them out to preach the kingdom of God and heal the sick.

(Luke 9:1–2)

This mission was not just for the original twelve apostles. When the seventy-two disciples were sent out in the next chapter, they were "to heal the sick" and announce that "the kingdom of God was near" (10:9), and when they returned, they were rejoicing because even the demons were submitting to them (10:17).

The expectation of the coming of the kingdom was a general hope for the Jews in Jesus's day. They had lived under siege for centuries. Jerusalem was not The City of Peace but a city of occupation. Many messianic communities developed in an attempt to bring in the kingdom. What most people expected was a unified political and geographical nation. Force and power were at the foundation of these expectations—to run out the oppressors. The common people were ready to accept Jesus as king; they, in fact, wanted to make him king by force (John 6:15). Jesus offered instead a kingdom not bound by geography or advanced by power— power at least as the Jews understood it in its political sense.

Jesus's kingdom was a spiritual kingdom, so it would not be obvious to those on the outside (Mark 4:11). It would be a realm of authoritative rule flowing from God Himself and embedded in His people wherever they went: "The kingdom of God is within[1] you" (Luke 17:20-21). This description is significant because it explains that the kingdom is not just an individual citizenship and privilege (though it goes with each of us) but is often most profoundly expressed in the community of the kingdom. It is a presence, described in terms of tiny things such as mustard seeds and yeast (Luke 13:18–21), both of which nonetheless bring large increase in the end. This kingdom is announced as here, but it is realized as yet to come (Matthew 25:34)—now but not yet.

In summary, Jesus reinstituted the rule or reign of God on earth through His people. It is the taking up of the laid-

---

1 Here, *within* could also be translated as *among*.

"So as I understand it, the kingdom of God is about the dynamic of God's kingship being applied . . . God's reign descends in and through Jesus and is applied in a world that is not fully under his authority. Sicknesses are healed, demons are banished, sins are forgiven and people are assured of God's love for them. Wherever God's kingdom comes, his kingship is applied and the evil of darkness is banished . . . it becomes clear that Jesus's death was not just to get individuals to heaven. It was to fix an entire creation that had been distorted by the Fall."

Allen Mitsuo Wakabayashi, *Kingdom Come*

down or forfeited authority that God had originally delegated to humanity. It was the turning point in the restoration process that is described in fullness in the Apocalypse of Revelations. This required Jesus to actively oppose the usurped authority structure that had been established through the forfeiture at Creation.

In 1 John 3:8, the apostle John writes, "The **reason** the Son of God appeared was to destroy the devil's work." This is a clear mission statement, and it helps us to understand what Jesus was contending for in announcing the kingdom. What was the work of the devil? Destruction. Defacement of the glory or image of God. Death. What God declared as good and very good at Creation took on the marks of destruction at the Fall. The evil work finds its strongest application in Satan's opposition to the redemption of humanity and restoration of creation itself. The apostle Paul ties the two together in Romans 8. Paul notes that creation itself, the raw stuff of our globe, has been groaning as in the pains of childbirth (8:22), that it waits for liberation from its bondage to death and decay (8:21), that it struggles in the frustration imposed on it (8:20), and that this expectation of liberation is wrapped up in the redemption of the children of God (8:19, 8:23).

Satan's works are multiple, but they can be summarized in two broad strokes. The first work is to keep people out of a relationship with God. 2 Corinthians 4:4 states, "The god of this age [Satan] has blinded the minds of unbelievers, so they cannot see the light of the gospel of the glory of Christ, who is the image of God." This echoes the Pauline calling, "to open their eyes and turn them from darkness to light, and from the power of Satan to God" (Acts 26:18). Here we are back to the image of the struggle between light and darkness.

Once that veil is lifted and people are rescued, the work of the enemy is to make life miserable or unfruitful for those who follow Christ. It is interesting that most of the references to the work of Satan in the Epistles are in relation to how he opposes the rescued Christ community. The apostle Peter calls the believers to alertness and self-control because "your enemy the devil prowls around like a roaring lion looking for someone to devour" (1 Peter 5:8). He goes on to exhort them to resist the devil. James calls the believer to a two-fold perspective—submit to God and resist the devil (James 4:7b). Jesus modeled how to do this in his use of authority.

Jesus and the Reinstitution of Authority

Jesus operated in his earthly ministry with authority. Always in submission to the Father's plan, Jesus thus knew from where that authority flowed:

I tell you the truth, the Son can do nothing by himself; he can only do what he sees the father doing. (John 5:19)

By myself I can do nothing . . . for I seek not to
please myself but him who sent me.

(John 5:30)

I do nothing on my own but speak just what the
Father has taught me.

(John 8:28)

For I did not speak on my own, but the Father who
sent me commanded me to say all that I have spoken.

(John 12:49)

"The words I say to you I do not speak on my own
authority. Rather, it is the Father, living in me, who
is doing his work."

(John 14:10)

Jesus clearly saw himself as an ambassador represent-
ing an authority greater than himself. Interestingly, the demons were never confused about his identity or authority
(Mark 1:24), and a "pagan" centurion also recognized Jesus's authority (Luke 7:1–10). It was the religious leaders
who refused to see Jesus's authority (Mark 11:27–33).

People observed Jesus's authority as a demonstration of
the advancement of the kingdom in several areas. First, he
taught with authority born from a source greater than personal knowledge (Mark 1:22) that contrasted with the authority

THE CHRIST EVENT AND AUTHORITY 43

of the teachers of the law. Though not officially recognized in the temple authority structure, Jesus's teaching and way of speaking packed an authoritative punch that the people were not used to experiencing in religious instruction (John 7:46). Second, the way that Jesus interacted with earthly authorities evidences a greater authority operating from heaven. He found himself in unruly and threatening crowds, but he simply slipped away. John explains that this was because Jesus's time had not yet come. When Jesus was on trial before Pilate he reminded the earthly ruler that he was operating through a vastly different kingdom structure: "My kingdom is not of this world." (John 18:36). Later, when Pilate challenged Jesus's silence by stating that he had power over Jesus's future in his hands, Jesus boldly declared, "You would have no power over me if it were not given to you from above" (John 19:11). Jesus clearly appeared to be powerless, yet he made a statement of authority.

Third, Jesus demonstrated his authority in his command over nature and destructive weather patterns that stemmed from a creation out of balance: "Who is this? Even the wind and the waves obey him!" (Mark 4:41). He exhibited a new level of authority in the magnitude of healing and deliverance that was released: "And Jesus healed many who had various diseases. He also drove out many demons" (Mark 1:34), and "He healed all who were ill" (Matthew 12:15). The response of the people demonstrates the incredible nature of Jesus's power:

The people were all so amazed that they asked each other, "What is this? A new teaching—and with authority! He even gives orders to impure spirits, and they obey him."

(Mark 1:27)

It is important that we begin here by acknowledging Jesus's earthly ministry as functioning in new patterns of authority that expressed the original design of the kingdom of God and not the social and cultural patterns of abusive authority and use of power. However, if we take a step back and view the entire Christ-event, we see that the reclaiming and further defining of that authority grows progressively in the unfolding of each stage: crucifixion, resurrection, and ascension.

Crucifixion. Colossians 2:15 describes the next step of the decisive victory of Jesus on the cross over the usurping authorities of the kingdom of darkness: "And having disarmed the power and authorities, he made a public spectacle of them, triumphing over them by the cross." Where Jesus operated with a new authority in his life and public ministry, he then in his death exposed, disarmed, and triumphed over the authority that Satan held since the Fall. We are reminded again of his reason for coming: "to destroy the works of the devil" (1 John 3:8). Simply, the atonement means that Jesus Christ took on the punishment for our sin. (See Romans 5 and 6 for further discussion by Paul.) Since the most obvious penalty of sin is death, the resurrection of Jesus speaks profoundly to the uniqueness of his death as triumphant victory. This victory is only possible in his identification with us as the God-man. Humans forfeited authority; Jesus is the new Adam, the only perfect human who takes the authority back. (See the insert box at the end of the chapter to understand how Jesus operates out of his humanity as the God-man.)

Resurrection. The Crucifixion would be meaningless without the affirmation of the Resurrection. Crucifixion alone makes Jesus merely a martyr. Resurrection was the Father's affirmation of the uniqueness of Jesus in His death on the cross. Jesus also came into a greater level of authority after the Resurrection. In Matthew 28:18, the Great Commission, he began, "All authority in heaven and earth has been given to me." Prior to the Resurrection, he described his work in light of the Father's authority. His declaration in Matthew 28:18 is interesting because of his designation of **all authority**. God does not need authority given to Him—everything flows from Him. Thus Jesus spoke as the resurrected God-man, our elder brother, not from out of his divinity. Through resurrection, the Son appears to have returned to a pre-incarnation level of authority. From this place of power, he passes authority on to us.

Ascension. At the Ascension, Jesus's authority was

solidified at the next level through his coronation to the throne of authority. Ephesians 1:19–23 shows this progression from resurrection to ascension:

> …His incomparably great power for us who believe. That power is the same as the mighty strength he exerted when he raised Christ from the dead and seated him at his right hand in the heavenly realms, far above all rule and authority, power and dominion, and every name that is invoked, not only in the present age but also in the one to come. And God placed all things under his feet and appointed him to be head over everything for the church, which is his body, the fullness of him who fills everything in every way.

The Ascension established Jesus over all authorities, rulers, powers, and dominions—who are positioned under his feet. Other biblical writers capture this transition in the alignment of authorities. Peter points to salvation being secured through the resurrected Christ, "who has gone into heaven and is at God's right hand—with angels, authorities, and powers in submission to him" (1 Peter 3:22).

Interestingly, the writer of Hebrews shows that though this is the positional reality—Christ is at the right hand of God and God's kingdom is on earth—there still remains the process of the people of God partnering with God to bring the kingdom to completion:

But when this priest had offered for all time one
sacrifice for sins, he sat down at the right hand of
God, and since that time he waits for his enemies to
be made his footstool.

(Hebrews 10:12–13)

Jesus triumphed over his enemies at the cross. The Resurrection validated his claim and restored another level of
authority. The Ascension positioned the authority. The Second Coming will establish the authority once and for all,
as every knee bows and every tongue confesses that He is
Lord to the glory of God the Father (Philippians 2:6–11).
However, we live in the in-between time, where we are to
exercise authority until all his enemies are brought to submission. As is stated repeatedly, the outcome of the war is
sure; we are simply winning battles in the unfolding of this
triumph.

To understand our role, we need to take the next step
of seeing how Jesus initially passed this authority on to his
followers and how in the Christ-event we too are in a place
to act with kingdom authority. Authority is delegated to
those who are called to exercise it for the good of others.

Jesus the God-Man

One of the mysteries of Christian doctrine is this notion of Jesus as the God-man. Historic, orthodox faith declares that in his incarnate state, Jesus was always God and always man. He was not a hybrid but fully both all the time. Thus any discussion about how he operated in power is laced with mystery.

Though he was always God, he somehow laid aside some of his divine capacity. The great Philippian hymn (Philippians 2:6–11) is one of the vital New Testament passages that develops our Christology. Paul appears to be quoting an early church hymn when he states that our attitude should be the same as that of Christ Jesus,

> Who being in very nature God, did not consider equality with God something to be grasped, but made himself nothing, taking the very nature of a servant, being made in human likeness...
> (2:6–7)

I want to emphasize one aspect of this declaration: "made himself nothing." Literally, the Greek says that "he emptied himself" (kenosis, κενοσισ). What I suggest is that somehow he took his divine prerogatives and suspended the use of them or set them aside for the sake of his mission as the incarnate Christ. Thus his identity was always the God-man but without full divine attributes of omnipotence, omniscience, or omnipresence.

This is clear on multiple levels. First, the eternal Son, in his incarnate body was not omnipresent. He was physically limited to his location. Second, he was not omniscient. When asked about the time of his return, he responded, "No one knows about the day or hour, not the angels, nor the Son, but only the Father" (Matthew 24:36). Third, he was not omnipotent. He took on the frailty of the human body, which would not restrain the eternal God.

So how did Jesus operate in power? I see him tapping into divine power through cooperation with the Holy Spirit. His public ministry did not begin until the descent of the Holy Spirit upon him at his baptism (Luke 3:21–22). Immediately after describing this event Luke writes, "Jesus himself was about thirty years old when he began his ministry" (3:23). Jesus made it clear as to how he operated with power: "by the Spirit of God" (Matthew 12:28) and "by the finger of God" (Luke 11:20). Luke describes Jesus's power not as one that Jesus exerted of his own will but one that was released at chosen times: "One day the power of the Lord was present for him to heal the sick" (Luke 5:17). The implication of this passage is that the previous day, or some other day, the power was not present. Peter makes the same point in a talk to a group gathered in the home of Cornelius:

> You know what has happened throughout Judea, beginning in Galilee after the baptism that John preached—how God anointed Jesus of Nazareth with the Holy Spirit and power, and how he went around doing good and healing all who were under the power of the devil, because God was with him.
>
> (Acts 10:37–38)

If Peter had wanted to declare that Jesus did his miracles as a sign of his divinity, he would not have emphasized the anointing by the Holy Spirit, and he would have more directly explained the miracles as "because he was God." I realize that John in his gospel puts an element of sign—pointing to Jesus's unique identity—in his description of the miracles. However, the flow of Jesus's power as described by the New Testament seemed to be initiated at his anointing by the Holy Spirit at baptism at the age of thirty, rather than as an ongoing element of his divine identity. Again, this is mystery.

In identity, Jesus is the God-man—always God, always man. He represents both sides of the covenant, divine and human. In bringing the kingdom of God, he appropriates power through the Spirit. He models for us how to operate in divine power to live beyond human weakness.

CHAPTER THREE

The Christ Follower and Authority

I t would be enough to know that our king has taken back the forfeited authority as the new Adam. However, the Bible takes the recovery a step further by highlighting how Jesus, the God-man, delegates the authority to his followers. We see this right from the beginning of Jesus's ministry.

Followers Authorized to Move in the Kingdom

Mark 6:7–13 depicts the initial sending of the twelve apostles. Jesus called this group to be with him as apprentices in the work of the kingdom (Mark 3:13–15). Before Jesus sent them, the text says that he "gave them authority" (6:7). This is the God way. At Creation, God gave authority away. At the start of re-creation Jesus works in the same way. The result is a similar, three-pronged ministry for followers: preaching, driving out demons, and healing (6:12–13).

Luke describes the same process in Luke 9:1–6. Some theologies have developed that suggest this divestiture of power was a special dispensation for the apostles. However, Luke tells us in the very next chapter that this same process occurs for the disciples, in addition to the apostles. An interesting dialogue occurs between Jesus and the seventy-two after they return from their journey of announcing the kingdom.

> The seventy-two returned with joy and said, "Lord, even the demons submit to us in your name." He replied, "I saw Satan fall like lightning from heaven. I have given you authority to trample on snakes and scorpions and to overcome all the power of the enemy; nothing will harm you. However, do not rejoice that the spirits submit to you, but rejoice that your names are written in heaven."
>
> (Luke 10:17–20)

The disciples held the same level of rulership as Jesus over demons. Jesus's response sets this notion of authority into the context of the brokenness of the created world and the powers of Satan: to overcome all the power of the enemy! Jesus seemed somewhat nonchalant about the whole process because this was what he expected for his followers. All the same, he warned his followers not to rejoice over the newfound resistance to power (the manifestation) but rather to celebrate the wellspring of that transaction (the relationship) and the guarantee that their names were written in heaven, a declaration of belonging in the kingdom.

To his immediate followers, Jesus passed on kingdom secrets from the Father: "Everything I have learned from my Father I have made known to you" (John 15:15). As a result, their commissioning took on the same characteristics of the Incarnation, minus the mysterious carrying of divinity in the God-man state: "As the Father has sent me, so I send you" (John 20:21). However, in John 14, the gospel writer points to how this commissioning extends beyond those who were physically present with Jesus in the first century:

> I tell you the truth, anyone who has faith in me will do what I have been doing. He will do even greater things than these, because I am going to the Father.
>
> (John 14:12)

Several elements of this passage are interesting to the discussion on moving in authority. Jesus offers the authority of the kingdom of God well beyond the original twelve or seventy-two, beyond the New Testament church, to **anyone**. A dispensational approach to authority and power will not work at this point. We cannot reject the miracles of Jesus and the Bible merely as conventions of an ancient world that attributed spiritual reasons for natural phenomena. Nor can we believe that the miracles and manifestation of the Holy Spirit are no longer needed now that we have God's Word.

We can see how this would play out in the interpretation of John 14:12. If your theology does not allow for the miraculous, then you would need to weave an interpretive dance around the idea of "greater things." One proposed explanation that I've heard of this passage attempts to reinterpret the delegated authority as unrelated to miracles by saying that the "greater things" refers to acts of love (which applies 1 Corinthians 13 to this declaration of Jesus). Even if this is the case, there is still the first phrase, "Anyone who has faith in me will do what I have been doing." We cannot get around the promise that we can act in authority, even to do miracles. We must always read Scripture in its immediate context. In verse 11, Jesus references the **"miracles themselves"** (John 14:11). Jesus did not do miracles as a kingdom of God sideshow. In performing them, he was restoring the rule and authority previously forfeited by humanity.

This notion of rulership is further explained or amplified in the Epistles through ideas such as inheritance, rights, overcomers, and conquerors. Romans 8 is a stirring passage of victory—not triumphalism—as it is set in the context of our struggle against sin (seen in Romans 7) and all things that seek to topple our faith: trouble, hardship, persecution, famine, nakedness, danger, sword, death, demons, powers, or anything else in creation (Romans 8). Against this backdrop of suffering and struggle, Paul calls us **joint heirs with Christ.** Heirs to what? We are heirs to every aspect of the Christ-life, including suffering but also operation in the power of the kingdom.

Paul describes this connection of authority and inheritance in Colossians 1 as well. In this letter to the holy and believing brothers and sisters in Christ, he begins with a long declaration of thanksgiving for the quality of life that flows from their new relationship in Christ. He then references the rights of their relationship "to share in the inheritance of the saints in the kingdom of light" (1:12). This inheritance came from Christ's rescue "from the dominion (exousia, εξουσια) of darkness" into the kingdom of the Son (1:13). The most casual reading of this passage captures the shifting of kingdom position and authority—**all rooted in a relationship with Christ.** Thus, authority is not a special endowment, calling, or gift to of a select few in the Christ family but the rightful inheritance of every believer.

The converse of this principle is seen in the story of the sons of Sceva (Acts 19:11–20). Luke tells the story of God doing "extraordinary miracles through Paul" in Ephesus and of those who try to copy his works.

> Some Jews who went around driving out evil spirits tried to invoke the name of the Lord Jesus.... One day the evil spirit answered them, "Jesus I know, and I know about Paul, but who are you?" Then the man who had the evil spirit jumped on them and overpowered them all. He gave them

such a beating that they ran out of the house naked
and bleeding.

(Acts 19:13a, 15–16)

The invocation of Jesus's name is not a talisman or
magic. It only works for those who have a relationship with
him. It is about our position in Christ, which was made possible in the Crucifixion and Resurrection. However, it gets
expressed most graphically for the Christ follower in the
position of rulership that Christ assumed in the Ascension.
Our recovered authority in our relationship with Christ is
most evident in the shared position of ascension.

The Believer's Authority and Position of Ascension

As noted previously in Chapter Two, within the pro-
gressive degrees of Christ's authority, the Ascension is
unique. Peter reminds believers, who were challenged on
every side and by all outward appearances losing the battle, that Jesus "has gone into heaven and is at God's right
hand—with angels, authorities, and powers in submission
to him" (I Peter 3:22). Paul makes this concept more real to
the follower of Christ by his unfolding of the implications
of this position in the letter to the Ephesians. He explains
that Jesus has realigned the structure of rulership so that all
powers and authorities come under his feet:

...His incomparably great power for us who believe. That power is the same as the mighty strength he exerted when he raised Christ from the dead and seated him at his right hand in the heavenly realms, far above all rule and authority, power and dominion, and every name that is invoked, not only in the present age but also in the one to come. And God placed all things under his feet and appointed him to be head over everything for the church, which is his body, the fullness of him who fills everything in every way.

(Ephesians 1:19–23)

This already is encouraging to those who feel the threatening presence of these other authorities, powers, and dominions, but Paul does not stop there. He continues in Chapter 2 by describing the impact of all this on the person who has been made alive in Christ. He describes a life before Christ as under the rule of Satan (2:2) and a life afterwards that exhibits signs of loyalty to a new kingdom. Then he reveals an important aspect of the believer's new position related to ascension: "And God raised us up with Christ and seated us with him in the heavenly realms in Christ Jesus" (2:6).

This is the pivotal verse on authority as it relates to the Christ follower. The tense used by Paul in this declaration is significant. Our instinct is to expect Paul to say that one day *we will be* seated with Him. That is the "not yet" expectation of the kingdom—longing for His kingdom to come! However, Paul uses the past tense: *raised* us up and *seated* us with Christ; these are completed actions. **We are seated with him.** Already done! Since those early believers who received the original letter from Paul were not already physically present at the throne of Jesus—nor are we—what was Paul saying? He was referring to our **spiritual** position. This means that in this intermediate time—the kingdom of "now but not yet"—authorities, powers, and dominions are underneath our feet. We are called to take up the authority reclaimed for us and bring to completion what Jesus established.

This helps us understand the intent of the writer of Hebrews in his description of completed enthronement—"sat down at the right hand"—and incomplete subjugation—"he waits for his enemies to be made his footstool" (Hebrews 10:12–13). From the perspective of spiritual authority, it is done. From the historical perspective, Christ followers are invited into the process of reigning with Christ by taking hold of this authority and reestablishing our rightful rule, His reign, on the earth. What the king declares, we the ambassadors execute in His name for the places and people that still remain outside of his rule.

So, What is the Authority of the Believer?

*Spiritual authority is the God-given right of ruler-
ship, rooted in a relationship with Him through Christ,
whereby we superimpose the rules, order, and impact of
His world (the kingdom of God) over our world.*

We return to the analogy of the traffic officer from the
preface. Authority trumps power. We have been recruited
to bring refreshed authority to a world that has gotten out
of balance and thus is not experiencing God's fullest blessing and abundance. We live in a world with all types of
competing authorities, powers, and dominions. Spiritual
authority in Christ trumps all of these. As these powers
come against us, we are to raise our spiritual hand and say
"No!" As these powers block the advance of God's kingdom, we are to exert our authority as ambassadors to accomplish the king's rule. This has multiple implications for
how we address the challenges of the flesh, the world, and
the devil. We will now move on to examples of how knowing our position in Christ and appropriating this authority
allows us to partner with God to impose His kingdom over
the kingdoms of this world.

CHAPTER FOUR

Authority Applied

S o what does it look like when we appropriate our authority? How does it change our lives and the lives of those around us? When we operate in authority, we superimpose the rule of God over the destructive rule of this present world. We pray for God's kingdom to come, and we exercise authority, and by doing so we participate in inviting and bringing His kingdom into our world. I do not perceive this as a passive desire but an active participation and partnership with God in His restoration program. For some, carrying out such power feels too bold and maybe even arrogant, and it would be, if this were not God's assignment—an assignment at which we failed originally but that has been restored to us through Jesus Christ. In the introduction, I noted three real examples of where I saw spiritual authority in operation. In this chapter, I will recount more examples from the categories of protection and cover, prevention and natural order, and provision and kingdom unleashing.

Protection and Cover

Protection and cover involve the active role that we play in our relationships, especially the situations where we have influence or authority. This authority could be determined by our social role, ascribed by others, or spiritually assigned to us (likely without others' knowledge). Our role is to take up this spiritual position of authority and to serve as an umbrella of protection over those we guard. We are to be servants in this role, delegated by God; our authority clearly flows from God, as do true protection and cover.

The Psalmist reminds us that the Lord is a fortress and a rock in whom we can take refuge (Psalm 94:22). A fortress is only valuable once you go inside it. A contemporary chorus declares, "The name of the Lord is like a strong tower; the righteous run into it and are saved." An older expression of this idea is the hymn "A Mighty Fortress is Our God," which describes God as a "bulwark never failing." A bulwark is a solid, wall-like structure raised for defense and protection. To call upon God as our bulwark is not just to passively take cover but to actively invoke a divine shield. God will not manipulate or force us to live under His umbrella of protection; He invites. We do not do this only for ourselves as individuals but are called to exercise protective authority for those under our influence and authority socially. I call this the gatekeeper role.

For example, I play an authoritative, protective role for my immediate family. I believe that the kingdom of darkness wants to bring destruction to these members under my care. In Jesus's teaching of the Good Shepherd (John 10:10), he warns of a thief who comes to steal, kill, and destroy. This is not a mere allegory. I have observed what I have come to believe as stratagems made against us to keep us from thriving and to block the work of God through us. It is very similar to what I noted early in the apostle Paul's words—Satan opposed me. We need to stand in authority against these demonic assignments by actively invoking our position behind the God bulwark.

When our family relocated to Mali, West Africa, our task was simple: to share the love of God with our Malian neighbors as it has been revealed and made accessible through Jesus Christ. Almost every one of our neighbors was Muslim, and they had been given false information about the identity and work of Jesus. They had reduced his role on earth to only that of prophet, missing the distinction of his role as Lord. As a result, they were cut off from a full understanding of who God is and how to be in dynamic and daily relationship with Him. One of the best places to make a connection was at Christmas time, because they do believe in the virgin birth. Thus we would hold virgin-birth celebrations at our home and use the gathering to share more truth about the gospel of the kingdom and how that gospel becomes complete through crucifixion and resurrection. We were ambassadors of God's love and witnesses in that community 365 days out of the year through word and deed, but Christmas Eve was vital for bold proclamation.

The first two years that we were in Mali, my wife, Ingrid, got very ill the week before the celebration. Because we were hosting these festive gatherings in our home, we had to cancel the events. Initially, I was annoyed at my wife. I was upset that she could not be stronger so that we could fulfill our calling to be active witnesses to Jesus Christ. Interesting how we can blame others for our own oversight! During this time I began to develop an understanding of the idea of spiritual gate-keeping. In hindsight, I believe that Ingrid's bouts of sickness were not merely physical ailments but spiritual attacks of the enemy against our family. So the following Christmas, I took my role seriously as protector of my family. I began early in the season verbally calling down spiritual covering over my family. I commanded against the plans of the kingdom of darkness to bring destruction to my family. In short, I was on alert and proactively took up my role as spiritual guardian for my family. God is really the one who protects—He is the fortress and refuge. But assigned to lead my family spiritually, I was entrusted by Him with the authority to protect. Ingrid was not sick any of the following Christmases. Now, I cannot prove that this was a result of my taking up my authority, but I have not laid down that responsibility since that time.

Does that mean that every time a member of my family is sick or experiences trouble that a demon is involved? No. We should be careful, especially as enlightened Christ followers, to avoid creating such extreme dichotomies in the face of spiritual principles. Part of the reason we may do so is that we have not developed a clear theology of suffering or an understanding of the ongoing impact of the Fall (paradise lost). Sometimes we are sick simply because of the biological or physiological realities of the world in which we live—a world that still groans for the redemption of all humans. Nevertheless, the spiritual world is not completely disconnected from the physical world, and there are times when the spiritual world plays out in physical realities. This is more in line with a holistic biblical view of reality than the Western convention of separating sacred and secular or spiritual and natural. In the same way that our theology is underdeveloped in the areas of power, it is also underdeveloped in the areas of suffering. I give a brief description of my understanding of suffering in the insert box below.

I have watched members of my congregation grab hold of this concept of authority, and it radicalized their prayers for their family. I can still feel the passion of a distraught mother who felt her marriage and children were under attack as they made decisions for the kingdom, so she prayed, "I'm not having it anymore!" Actively invoking the Divine bulwark immediately brought relief and a sense of peace. I will never forget the father who stood at the front door of his house issuing commands into the night as we anointed the doorposts with oil. There had been manifestations of evil in their home at night with objects moved and photos turned upside down. As he stood in authority at the front door he changed the spiritual climate of his household. I will always be gripped by the prayer of a friend after a quick, five-minute explanation of authority and her role as spiritual gatekeeper—even for her adult child, who kept making bad choices. She brought every resource of the kingdom of God into that struggle. Protection and cover—for ourselves and for the ones that we are called to protect, in the lines of natural and spiritual authority of the world in which we live.

This can go beyond our family authority structure to the places where we have influence in our work and community. Recently I had a discussion with a man in my church who works as the leader of a team in a financial institution. When he was hired to this position, from outside the corporation, he found a fragmented team and a toxic work atmosphere. Having heard me teach on taking authority in our places of influence, from day one in this new position, he began praying the Lorica of St. Patrick (see Appendix 3) over his own desk and prayer walking the entire office. He further made a conscious effort to take an interest in the lives of his team members and even initiated prayer with them when the opportunity arose. He also launched a strategic king-

Initial Reflection on a Theology of Suffering

When I tell stories about God's intervention of power to change a situation, some might be tempted to press my message to an illogical extreme by suggesting that if we then wield our God-given authority, we will never suffer. This conclusion is not biblical, nor have I seen it bear out in real life. Even my family has still experienced sickness and trial since those Christmases in Bamako. Because I do not want to encourage an imbalanced practical theology, I have given much thought to the issue of suffering and have come to identify four types of suffering.

First, there is suffering common to humanity living in a fallen creation. As noted earlier, even creation (the earth) groans for the redemption of the sons of man. There are natural places of pain in our lives from being on a deteriorating globe, including those attached to human aging. This is the impact of sin in general.

Second, there is suffering as a result of the consequences of our or others' specific sins. For example, if I abuse alcohol and drive intoxicated, I could end up injuring or even killing someone else. This is suffering as a result of practiced sin.

Third, there is suffering assigned by God to bring a greater glory to the name of Jesus. The apostle Paul declares, "I want to know Christ and the power of his resurrection and the fellowship of sharing in his sufferings, becoming like him in his death" (Philippians 3:10). My observation of history is that the kingdom of God advances with two types of impact—power and suffering. On the boundaries between the faith community and the not-yet faith community is often an explosion. Sometimes God releases unusual seasons of miracles and interventions to validate the message. More often, God's servants are given the privilege to suffer, and their response of grace and hope is more convincing than even the miracles. This is a hard concept for Americans to grasp because we have created a God in our own image—a God who makes us feel good rather than a God who invites us to share in His restoration project and to become victors in the pattern of Jesus.

Fourth, there is suffering that is the attacks of the enemy as stealer, killer, and destroyer. If we are fruitful in partnering with God to bring His kingdom to this world, Satan loses territory in his falsely taken role as ruler of this age, and more importantly, we take back the spoils of what is so precious to God—people rescued from the kingdom of darkness and brought into the light. To echo the calling of the apostle Paul, "Turn them from darkness to light, and from the power of Satan to God" (Acts 26:18). Somehow even this fits into the sovereign plan of God, although in these situations His assignment for us is to resist.

I can only act to relieve the suffering of the second and

fourth categories. While I cannot control others or the potential of their sin affecting my life, I can be a steward of my own life so that I do not cause others to suffer through my actions. Likewise, I certainly do not want to come under the attacks of the enemy. I can act as spiritual gatekeeper for my family and others who are under my influence and authority; I do not want to leave them exposed because of spiritual passivity. For the other two types of suffering, I can only accept the suffering of our world and the suffering that God assigns to bring His glory.

As I reflect on these four categories of suffering, I realize that they are merely descriptive—and not neat descriptions at that. There is a mystery in how suffering gets enveloped into our life stories in a way that is redemptive in God's sovereign plan. I could recount numerous situations for each category in which those who suffered tell a story of God's redemption and blessing through the suffering. The obvious challenge is that so many instances of suffering seem so arbitrary from our present vantage point.

My biggest concern in building a theology of suffering alongside an understanding of the authority of the believer is that we do not develop a presumptuous application of our authority. Our authority is not a guarantee against pain or trouble. Again, this pushes us back to embrace the most important aspect of the discussion—a relationship with God, rather than the use of His power.

dom of God invasion by placing the cross on his own wall and leaving his Bible and other Christian literature out on his desk. His combination of leading as a kingdom servant and standing in kingdom authority changed the spiritual climate of the workspace and the effectiveness of his team. He changed the natural reality of his work world through spiritual means.

Prevention and Natural Order

When Jesus walked on the earth, he was able to change the natural world through spiritual command. Some followers of Christ today might feel comfortable with the idea of protecting our families or those over whom we have influence or authority, but would feel that it is taking it too far to suggest we can change natural order. Yet in the same way that Jesus had authority over nature, we too can exercise our authority against the natural order when the advancement of the kingdom is at stake. I will highlight two poignant situations from my own life as concrete examples of where I observed the power of spiritual authority over natural order, in the face of what appeared to be opposition or even disaster. I cannot prove that the results directly correlated to the exercise of authority, but this is my experience. Faith is not rational. Conversely, it is not irrational. It is trans-rational. Faith experiences are laced with mystery. Nonetheless, in the words of William Temple, Archbishop of Canterbury (1942–1944), "When I pray, coincidences happen, and when I don't, they don't." In relation to my authority as a Christ follower, my experiences point to the value of taking a proactive stand and declaring my position in Christ.

The first instance occurred when I was a teenager. We were traveling home from Sunday evening church. My dad was driving. We were traveling south on Interstate 71 when we crested a long hill. From the back seat, I alerted my father that something was happening at the bottom of the hill. We were about to discover that black ice had formed on the roadway and cars were spinning out of control at the bottom of the hill. My father began applying the brakes but to no avail; in fact, we continued to descend the hill with more speed and less control, barreling down on cars that had careened off of the road. In the confusion, people had begun leaving their cars, and we were headed right for one car where the family had gotten out. We were not only going to smash into their car, we were going to crush them in the process. My mother put her hand on the dashboard and declared, "Jesus save us!" In my memory, we came to an immediate stop, only yards from the family. While I cannot prove that her cry controlled the situation, our car had seemed physically impossible to stop.

The second event occurred in Mali. We were in a season of active evangelism in the *quartier* of Daoudabougou. God had been releasing a number of kingdom manifestations, including healing, deliverance from evil spirits, and people entering into relationship with Him through Jesus Christ. It was all God, but his agent of ministry was an evangelist from Burkina Faso, who would preach and then invite people to be healed. God was at work, and through the testimony of people who experienced this healing, expectant crowds began to gather to meet God, or at least see His power released. The evening that I remember, our little church courtyard had over one thousand people assembled to hear the name of Jesus lifted up. The choir was singing in preparation for the preaching and ministry when a violent storm began to roar. The wind that howled in front of the rain clouds not only hurled the red dust of the Mali soil, it was bending over the poles that held banners and sound equipment. When storms arise in this fashion, people flee with similar violence.

I stepped to the back of the courtyard with my son, who was around seven years old. We knelt under a mango tree, put our hands in the air, and commanded the storm to cease. Slowly the wind came to a standstill, and we continued with our announcement of the gospel of the kingdom. I doubt I was the only one praying, for we had other Malian Christ followers at this event. However, when we left Daoudabougou that evening, we realized the nature of the intervention. In all directions from the church courtyard was significant damage from the storm. Large puddles lined the roads, but the area within a kilometer of the church was untouched—literally dry. Coincidence? I cannot *prove* that this was a miracle over nature but all the signs point to it.

In both of these accounts from my life there is an underlying principle. In each case, the intervention resulted in bringing God glory and restoring relationships to Him—not merely making our lives more comfortable. In the first situation, the family getting out of the car was our neighbor. The seeming miracle of our car coming to a sudden halt propelled an ongoing conversation between my mother and the other woman about faith. It led to the family deciding to enter into an active relationship with God through Christ. Likewise, the miraculous nature of the intervention in Daoudabougou restored many people to their relationship with God. In each case, the resulting opportunity to proclaim Christ's glory made the moments more significant than simply praying for a safe trip or for pleasant weather for a picnic or softball game. Again, we need to remind ourselves that we are not turning God into the dispenser of good fortune at our every beckoning. These interventions are always a part of His restoration project.

I don't claim to know how this works. I do not presume that these are automatic results of taking spiritual authority. I can only control that which already aligns with God's design. This is the same principle as binding and loosing in Scripture: "What has been bound in heaven will be bound on earth" (Matthew 16:19). I have prayed with authority at other times that seemed just as important and not seen similar results. I do not know where God's sovereignty ends and the rule of the prince of this world takes up. I don't know exactly where I stand in the midst of those two opposed kingdoms. I do not know when what I regard as obviously important for the advancement of the Gospel is just my well-intended desire. But I have come to recognize the difference of standing passively between those competing realities and taking an active stand in Jesus's name. And I have moved to a point in my journey where I've stopped trying to figure it all out. I command from my position, in Jesus's name, knowing that God will only release that which aligns to His way. I do not want to miss His way by being silent.

Provision and Kingdom Unleashing

There are kingdom manifestations or benefits that also touch our lives as we take hold of our spiritual authority. These include wholeness, healing, freedom, and blessing— what I would term divine interventions to change the natural order. We are reminded by Jesus to have a right order in seeking these things. "But seek first his kingdom and his righteousness, and all these things will be given to you as well" (Matthew 6:33). Jesus declares this in the midst of teachings about having the right treasures in life and not worrying about daily provision. We might assume that he is saying to just tolerate life when it does not work the way we want. However, this assumption does not fit the context; Jesus brackets the passage on worry with two clear teachings about bold prayer, where we are commanded to ask boldly for kingdom benefits to come. When we understand our spiritual authority it brings the asking into the larger context of restoring God's kingdom to our world. In the introduction, I told the story of the parents who were distraught because their son would wake up with terrible nightmares. This went on for a long period of time. No amount of practical care brought results. Then they secretly anointed his bedroom with oil and took up their authority as spiritual gatekeepers of the household. That finally brought newfound peace at nighttime for the family.

Shortly after this event, I was teaching in Australia, and I used their testimony to talk about consecrating people, places, and things to the Lord through the act of anointing with oil. I explained that our confidence is not in the oil, nor even our ability to pray. The oil is an outward sign that mobilizes inward faith and also makes a declaration to the spirit world. The key is to know our position in Christ and to anoint in full awareness of our authority.

After the teaching, a young man came up to me. His young son had not been able to speak and struggled to put words together in a comprehensible manner. This created all types of frustration for him and for his family. The young man asked, "Could it be an assignment of evil, and what should I do?" I advised him to anoint his son's bedroom and the boy as well while he slept, without his son's knowledge.

A couple weeks later I received the following e-mail:

The day after the seminar, we, as a family, prayed over and anointed our home, as well as our children. We felt a leading to specifically pray over our 2½-year-old, asking the Lord to loosen his tongue, as he has not been able to communicate properly, causing much frustration, tantrums, and concern on our part. Throughout the following week we witnessed a dramatic change in speech. He began to communicate effectively, learning new words— hourly!! Something we had not experienced with him up until that point. Praise God and thank you for sharing your insight and own experiences.

I could tell dozen of accounts of what happens when we take authority against the work of the kingdom of darkness in the lives of people around us. I have been involved in deliverance ministry for about twenty-five years. The first time that a demon spoke to me through another person, I was not prepared, I had no training to know how to guide that person into inner healing and deliverance. I was firmly grounded in the word of God, so I believed in a dark spirit world that opposed us, but I had no experiential knowledge on how to respond to that world. I held a more defensive approach rather than an offensive approach to setting people free.

I was becoming a kingdom theologian and beginning

to understand the notion of my authority in Christ. Now I realize that it was God preparing me, in my ignorance, to actually live out His full calling in my life—to preach the kingdom, to heal the sick, and to cast out demons. I believe this is not the calling of a select few, but the inheritance of all those in a relationship with God through Jesus Christ.

On that first encounter twenty-five years ago, with no training, yet positioned in Christ with authority and led by the Holy Spirit, I cast out three demons from that young woman. That evening I recognized without question how far more powerful the demons were than me, but I also saw how my authority from God trumped their power. The spirits made an intimidating show, but I had a sense of control of the situation, and they came to attention each time I addressed them because I spoke in the name of Jesus. Prior to the deliverance, when the young woman looked in a mirror, she saw demons, and when she attended worship services, the music was a clanging noise in her mind. After the deliverance, she saw her own eyes in the mirror, and she was enveloped in joy and peace during worship.

Since that first deliverance session, I have walked hundreds of people through separation from the spirits that were tormenting them and making their lives more difficult than was necessary. These attachments and influences ranged from chronic problems to annoying setbacks. I have walked myself through guided prayers of cleansing from the past. I have watched others take the authority and do the same for themselves and others. And I have seen the fruit of transformed lives afterwards. At the foundation of each of these stories is the repossession of our calling to exercise authority in this world.

Likewise, the provision of blessing has unfolded in multiple ways through active, authoritative prayer. I've watched people pray for the selling of their home—on the market for over a year—and the house go into contract the next day. Again, intervention and blessing are not a guaranteed response; they always flow within the structure of what God is doing. In one instance of a house on a market for a long time, the homeowners were active in their faith and had a strong practice of intercessory and supplication prayer. I would even have called them prayer warriors. Even so, immediately after they heard my teaching on spiritual authority, they prayed with a new sense of authority—and received an offer on the house in the next day and closed in record time. In that situation, they appear to have overcome some kind of opposition to their provision.

I once had a visiting minister pray over me with authority to break a financial curse that had been placed on me through a previous ministry I had served. The minister knew nothing about the details of my story beyond that I was a pastor. What he did not know was that I had extensive debt due to multiple factors, in particular poor decisions by an accountant for three years that resulted in my needing to pay three years' worth of underpaid taxes. As the minister prayed over me, he discerned this financial curse, broke it with authority, and declared that a change was coming. He prayed on a Saturday; the following week I was given $24,000, and within a few months another $12,000—a significant burst toward the process of eliminating our debt. I cannot prove that his use of authoritative commands in prayer was connected to the unexpected provisions, but it does seem an odd coincidence.

I want to stress that I am not a "name it and claim it" theologian. God is not the owner of the great candy shop in the sky waiting for us to ask so that He can dole out goodies. I do believe that God is Jehovah Jireh, "the Lord who sees" or "the Lord our provider" (Genesis 22). I do believe that every good and perfect gift comes from the Father above (James 1:17). I do believe in the principles of hard work and faithful stewardship of this provision. It is not God's primary purpose for me to be rich, in the financial sense, as some "name it and claim it" theologians suggest. (See my section on suffering above.) God wants me to be spiritually rich in Jesus—and that is His desire for everyone. If I am to become financially rich, it is so that I can give as much away as possible. I want to avoid the extreme swing of the pendulum of practiced theology as I try to reconnect people to their authority in Christ.

I have watched areas of a town or a region open up to the gospel after people took to the streets, taking their authority in prayer. In Mali I observed a people that had resisted the good news of the kingdom for over seventy years—even while their brothers (the same tribe) across the border in Burkina Faso had responded to the gospel in large numbers. Likewise, some of the surrounding tribes in Mali had responded affirmatively to this good news and had experienced fruitfulness, yet this one group remained resistant. This all changed when a group of women spent a week in fasting and prayer, with a new sense of authority in Christ, before an evangelism team came to spend a week in the village to talk about Jesus and his kingdom. Everything changed that week. This was not the first attempt at reaching this village, but it was the first attempt with success. A new, small congregation was born in the wake of this authoritative prayer and faithful witness. Again I cannot prove that this resulted from the prayers of those women, but the coincidence seems rather large.

The same conversion happened in the town of Nyack, New York. One of the college-led gospel teams had spent seven years in witness with no conversion fruit. Then a group of students in a class were mobilized to take their authority in prayer to the streets. For a week, they saturated the community with prayer. That Friday night, three people responded affirmatively to active witness on the streets. Coincidence? Could be. But even a skeptical mind may make a connection: seven years, no success; one week of intensive prayer, immediate success. My life experience and observation is that when people pray with authority, the blessings of God's kingdom seem to be released with greater impact. Is there a better blessing than people moving from the kingdom of darkness to the kingdom of light? We harken back to the words of Jesus, "Don't rejoice that the demons respond to you in my name, rejoice that your names are written in heaven" (Luke 10:20) Faith experience is preserved as narrative in the form of testimony. Faith never can be "proven" in a scientific sense but all sharing of history or event is subjected to same sense of subjective retelling. It is difficult for me to know which stories to tell. There are so many. Does this mean that I have not had trouble in my life? Absolutely not! At times I have taken a strong, authoritative stand over my flesh, bringing it under my spiritual authority as one crucified with Christ. At other times I have failed to step up and have acted on that carnal desire. At times I have taken a strong authoritative stand against the systems of this world that are moving against my spiritual progress and the community of faith that I serve. At others times I have been complicit in simply going with the flow. The result was that God's blessing did not flow with the same intensity. At times I have put a flag into the ground, announcing to the kingdom of darkness that my family was off limits. At other times I was caught off guard, not using discernment, even after years of recognizing darkness around me. But it all somehow gets wrapped up into the journey of becoming an overcomer in Christ Jesus. In the process, I am learning to reign with him as a joint heir. In the end, it really boils down to my relationship with God through Jesus and my active partnership with Him to see Jesus glorified as king as I help others enter into the fullness of that relationship as well. Let me mention again, "Rejoice that your names are written in heaven" {Luke 10:20).

One of the immediate responses of the call to use of authority is of concern for the potential for misuse. The mishandling of our authority is always possible. Nonetheless, in the same way that I do not avoid the fire of the Holy Spirit only because some have used it incorrectly, I do not avoid walking in my authority because of the potential of its misuse. This brings us to some important principles in the use of our Christ-positioned authority.

CHAPTER FIVE

Practical Guidelines

Spiritual authority is a function of relationship and position, not of performance. It is not a result of spiritual maturity, though the more mature we become and the more comfortable with our Christ identity, the more we will be prepared to appropriate our authority. It is not to be equated with a filling by the Holy Spirit. We know that fullness of the Holy Spirit is a daily practice that makes the Christ-life possible. We must daily refill with the Holy Spirit because we "leak." Authority, on the other hand, does not ebb and flow like anointing by the Holy Spirit, because our spiritual authority is linked to our position in Christ. This suggests that our authority as believers is not equated with the depth or quality of our spiritual walk. Sometimes we might be in a bad place spiritually, yet we can still take a stand with great effect based on our position in Christ. However, in those times the enemy of our soul, who is called the "accuser of believers" (1 Timothy 4:13, Revelation 13), will challenge our sense of security and cause us to doubt our position or standing. Given this reality, it is important to remember that our authority will flow most fluidly when other aspects of our lives are aligned to

God's way. Thus it is wise to learn the principles behind a consistent use of authority so that we can operate without a sense of complicity or hesitation.

The Ambassador Principle

In the same way that authority and rulership were assigned to us at Creation, they are delegated to us anew in re-creation. Jesus is the king, and the force behind our authoritative stand is his kingdom. He entrusts that authority to us as stewards or ambassadors. Ambassadors have no power of their own. They can only represent the sovereignties that have commissioned the ambassadors to act on their behalf. The apostle Paul applied this concept to our calling as ministers of reconciliation: "We are therefore Christ's ambassadors, as though God were making His appeal through us" (2 Corinthians 5:20).

Thus, one of our essential tasks is to align our will with that of the Father so that we are exercising authority as He desires. Jesus was quite clear: I do what the Father is doing, I go where the Father is going, I speak what I hear from the Father. Does what I am seeking to do with my authority line up with God's will? Is it what the Father wants? This means discerning the Father's timing as well. We might be impressed to take kingdom action that makes perfect sense with all that we know about God and His desire to restore the kingdom. Nonetheless, if it is not His time, we might mistakenly force the issue and end up with an even less desirable result. The operative word is *"relationship,"* which ensures a flow of communication that is born out of intimacy. The ambassador needs to keep open the lines of communication to the sovereign.

The Community Principle

Not only are we to exercise authority in submission to the Father, but we are to use it in submission to others, especially those in the Christ community. The rediscovery of our spiritual authority has an amazing impact. All of a sudden, we see God work through the word of our command with such ease where before seemed only struggle. As Jesus did, we begin to move with an attitude that announces "The kingdom of God is here!" With these results, our confidence grows. We must subsequently be careful that our confidence is rooted primarily in our position with God; confidence rooted in performance or results can cause us to become conceited.

One common mistake is to assume that **we alone** know the mind of God and what He intends for every situation. I see this narrow mindset and subsequent arrogance both in individuals and in branches of the faith community (i.e., denominations). We must apply our authority with an attitude of mutual submission to other members of the body of Christ. Doing so keeps us from becoming self-congratulatory, spiritual monopolies. The idea of mutual submission leads naturally into the next principle, humility.

The Humility Principle

Since authority is not about performance, rather only about stewardship, nothing in its application is self-exalting. The use of our authority is not to impress people or toshow off spiritually. Our security and self-image flow from knowing who we are in Christ, not from a remarkable ministry. At the core of this realization is a wholeness of life, where we understand that all advancement in life is a result of God working in and through us, not a result of our performance. I like Father Richard Rohr's expression, "Nothing to prove, nothing to protect." When we operate from this foundation we feel no compulsion to be recognized by others when God works through us.

When the seventy-two disciples return to Jesus and report the impact of their newfound authority, Jesus is rather nonchalant in his response. "I have given you authority"—i.e., "I expected you to see manifestation of the kingdom."He then reminds them not to rejoice in the manifestation or impact but to find their sense of joy in that their names were written in heaven. Our relationship and position with God is far more important than what we can do in His name.

I have heard some people use this same passage to limit

the use of our authority, concluding that God does not want us to exercise authority, just to rejoice in the relationship with God. This passivity was not Jesus's intent. Likewise, a reflexive false humility causes some to be afraid of using their spiritual authority: *How can we assume to act so boldly in Jesus's name?* Whereas some Christ followers find it presumptuous to operate with such boldness in the face of the enemy of our soul, I consider the failure to do so prideful rebellion, much like when we originally forfeited God's assignment to us to rule. One of my students wrote it this way:

It is a rejection of Christ to live in fear and not accept the authority that God gives me in Christ . . . Christ did not overcome death to have no meaning or power . . . Therefore, I have a vested responsibility to speak God's word, binding the futile works of Satan, and [to] live in ways that are a realization of God's victory and Christ's reign.

The Love Principle

Authority misused makes God angry. Authority must always flow in a stream of His love. It is not meant to benefit the powerful, nor can it be used to hurt the powerless. Only shortly after the apostles used authority to bring healing (Luke 9:1–6), they wanted to use it to punish people in a Samaritan village that did not welcome Jesus (Luke 9:51–

55) by calling down fire from heaven. But Jesus rebuked them. Interestingly, the Greek verb translated as "rebuked" (επιτιμαω) is the same verb used to describe Jesus's command to the evil spirit that had afflicted a man (Luke 4:35). Jesus disapproves of our abuse of spiritual authority with the same passion that he holds against demonic destruction.

Somehow God's sovereign authority has the ability to guard the dignity of people by honoring their free will. He is compelling but not manipulative in His power and authority. God honors the integrity of those whom He approaches. He will not force the blessing that flows from His authority onto people. This is seen in the movement of Jesus, who operated in life-changing authority; healing and deliverance flowed out from Him. Nevertheless, when he returned to his hometown, "he could not do any miracles there, except lay his hands on a few people and heal them" (Mark 6:5). Mark tells us that he was amazed by their lack of faith (6:6). Underneath that message is the notion that God does not force His benefits on people. They either choose the way of blessing or decide to remain under the impact of the curse. Love invites and holds the *other* with a great sense of dignity.

The Kingdom Focus Principle

We are not to seek authority but to seek the king instead. It is easy to focus on revealing the kingdom and make the manifestation the goal. Rather, the purpose is to glorify the king through a deepened relationship with Him—to know Christ! We can become so enamored with the manifestation of the Holy Spirit that we miss the greatest blessing, which is the sense of God's intimate presence through the indwelling of the Spirit. The longer I walk with God, the more I relish in what I consider His greatest promise: "I am with you!" or "I will never leave you!" Interestingly, this promise often follows the most frequent command of Scripture, "Fear not!" All the other benefits of His promises are good, but the sense of His manifested presence is the best. As David cries out in repentance, "Do not cast me from your presence or your Spirit from me" (Psalm 51:11).

Bobby Clinton, in *The Making of a Leader*, has suggested a similar approach to leadership: "A leader does not seek spiritual authority; a leader seeks to know God." Knowing God—having a relationship with him—guarantees a position of authority. When we seek first the king and his kingdom, we can live with assurance that His presence will be equal to any situation we face.

This is important because in the Scriptures it is clear that God often brings confirmation of the message of his servants through the manifestation of the kingdom. When John the Baptist sent his followers to affirm Jesus's identity as the Messiah, they asked, "Are you the one?" Jesus responded, "Go back and report to John what you hear and see" (Matthew 11:2–4). What they heard and saw was the demonstration of the kingdom. The apostle Paul declared, "My message and my preaching were not with wise and persuasive words but with a demonstration of the Spirit's power" (1 Corinthians 2:4). The translation of this verse does not capture the intensity of Paul's expectation of demonstration. The Greek is literally "spirit and power" (πνευ–ματοσ και δυναμασ). Furthermore, in telling the story of the early church, Luke repeatedly points to the confirmation of God's hand through signs and wonders as vital to the spread of the Word of God; see the stories of Philip (Acts 8:6), Peter (Acts 10), and Barnabas and Saul (Acts 14:3).

All of these examples of the early Christ followers witnessing miracles can cause us to feel as though somehow we are not matching up. This has caused some to develop cessationist theologies, which suggest that signs and wonders are not for today. This explanation displays an unfortunate, rather shallow view of the Word. First, when we look at the chronology of the Bible, we see that often, during the life of a spiritual leader, large periods of time went by between prodigious acts of God. It may be only 1/8–inch of white space in the Bible separating these divine events, but it may be twenty years in the life of the servant of God. Only Jesus seems to emanate regular, if not daily, kingdom manifestation. Secondly, our call is to be faithful and allow God to be fruitful through our faith. Paul states it this way: some plant, some water, but it is only God who can bring the increase (1 Corinthians 3:5–9). This points to the importance of seeking the kingdom foremost and trusting God that His manifestation and demonstration of the kingdom, in whatever form, is sufficient for the moment.

The Wholeness Principle

Spiritual authority flows most fully when we are most whole. One question often posed to me is why Jesus seemed to have such a strong flow of kingdom authority, while it seems to be more of a dribble for us. When we look at the accounts of his three years of earthly ministry, they are packed with divine manifestations. Jesus healed many, he drove out many demons, all the sick and demon-inflicted from a village were brought to him (Mark 1:32–34), and people sought him out as their only hope. So why are manifestations more limited for us?

Jesus was fully human, like us. The writer of the epistle to the Hebrews notes, "He had to be made like his brothers in every way…that he might make atonement for the sins of the people" (Hebrews 2:17). However, Jesus lived out his earthly life with one big difference—he was not born with original sin and he did not practice sin. He took on weakness, human limitation, and even the challenge of temptation, just like us. The writer of Hebrews reminds us that though tempted as us in every way, Jesus was "yet without sin" (4:15).

I like to use the image of a pipe to explain the difference (see diagrams below). Using the pipe image, we can see that authority flows from God for both Jesus and us. God's authority is not to be pooled or contained but is to be allowed to flow. In the case of Jesus, the flow was unrestricted (Image 1). In contrast, when authority flows into us it finds a number of blockages—original sin, practiced sin, wounds that develop from our own sin and sin committed against us, false beliefs, and so on (Image 2). The more that our lives are cleansed of these obstructions, the easier the flow of authority and the greater the force (Image 3). Jesus takes the problem of sin on himself at the cross. When we agree to allow him to bear our sin, our problems from sin from birth and in practice becomes rectified. Christ became sin so that we might become righteous—right before God. Our pipeline is cleaned out.

Each time we sin again we can return in confession for a fresh cleansing. Beyond the cleansing, sin loses its power over us, and we have strength to live out a new identity in holiness. Holy living keeps the pipe from filling up again. There might still be the consequences or wounds from past sin, both those which we have committed or had perpetrated against us. Inner healing removes the attachments to past wounds. With each experience and level of healing, the pipe becomes more open to the onrush of kingdom authority.

This image is not intended to encourage us to try to do more or perform more to facilitate the flow of authority. This gets the process backwards. Seek first the king and His kingdom. It is in an intimate relationship that we see our-

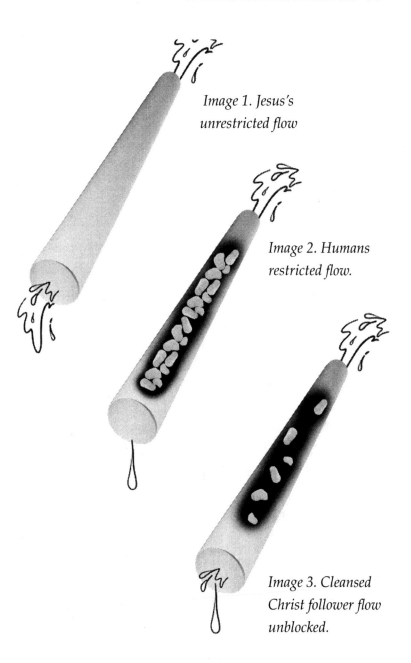

Image 1. Jesus's unrestricted flow

Image 2. Humans restricted flow.

Image 3. Cleansed Christ follower flow unblocked.

selves as we truly are and that we allow His wholeness to become our personal reality. With wholeness comes a natural flow of His divine power.

The Earthly Authority Alignment Principle

So what is the connection between spiritual authority and earthly authorities? A clear parallel is not always apparent, but alignment of earthly authority to spiritual authority brings strength. Spiritual authority always trumps other authorities. This is clearly indicated in Jesus's response to Pilate (John 19:11). All authorities flow ultimately from God. When authorities collide, the ethic of the kingdom always takes precedence. Therefore, at times Jesus reminds his followers to honor political structures, while at other times he openly challenges the political and religious authorities.

The apostle Paul carries this notion further by calling us to submit to earthly authorities, even when they are not operating in complete obedience to God (Romans 13:1–7). The apostle Peter calls for the same submission (1 Peter 2:13–17). Additionally, both point to the flow of authority in family structures, particularly in the marriage relationship (Ephesians 5:22–33, 1 Peter 3:1–7). These instructions need to be understood in the context of the ethic of Christ's kingdom, in which authority is never used to manipulate but to serve and protect.

In the same manner as the wholeness principle, when

earthly authorities align and cooperate with spiritual authority, the flow of divine authority is greater. I will give an example from my own life. I am in submission to Jesus as king over my life and over all areas of my life that extend influence over others. Out of the flow of his authority, I am to exercise authority at all times, most importantly in the areas where my personal influence impacts others. First, I consider myself a spiritual gatekeeper for my immediate family. In that sense, I exercise authority to close the spiritual gates against the kingdom of darkness and to open the gates to the kingdom of light. I stand on the rampart monitoring the flow of blessing and curse (Deuteronomy 28). When my family members agree to and cooperate with this authority structure, they experience a greater flow of God's authority and reveal the presence of the kingdom in their own places of influence. My children are adults now and do not need to stay under my authority, but it is to their advantage. When they were children, they were blessed by being obedient. Now that we are in adult relationships, they are blessed by honoring me, even if not necessarily called to obey me. Even as they develop their own sense of spiritual authority and exercise that authority for the sake of others, they can align themselves to the spiritual guardianship that I offer them.

All of the areas in life in which I have influence or leadership can have a similar level of alignment. As a pastor, I also keep watch for my spiritual family. They are blessed by honoring that structure. This is not oppressive but liberating, as long as I lead as a servant and not for self gain. This makes the instructions in Hebrews come alive.

> Remember your leaders, who spoke the Word of God to you. Consider the outcome of their way of life and imitate their faith.
>
> (Hebrews 13:7)

> Obey your leaders and submit to their authority. They keep watch over you as men who must give an account. Obey them so their work will be a joy, not a burden, for that would be of no advantage to you.
>
> (Hebrews 13:17)

The character of leadership and the benefit of followership are both expressed in these verses.

My wife and I have rewritten and memorized the Lorica of St. Patrick (see Appendix 3), and we recite it in prayerful declaration as spiritual gatekeepers and releasers of authority for areas and people under our influence and leadership. The prayer is filled with declarations of protection under God and the finished work of Jesus, and it closes with this phrase: "As I move into this day, I appropriate all this for myself and for all who are under my authority and influence." To me this is not just a ritual but an alignment of authority structures. I take this responsibility very seriously.

With this recognition of alignment, I recognize that we are called at times to challenge earthly authorities. Our ultimate allegiance is to the kingdom of God. When faced with compromise, we should choose the kingdom ethic of Jesus. Daniel and his friends in the Old Testament chose civil disobedience over the idolatry of bowing before a king. Jesus challenged manipulative religious authorities. A more recent example is Martin Luther King, Jr., when he stood against the sin of racism practiced by society and protected by government authorities and laws. Crucially, his prophetic stand was done in an ethic of the kingdom: nonviolent resistance. This was real authority embedded in the principle of love, and it resulted in the changing of the laws and some attitudes toward a more righteous understanding of humanity for our nation. We still have a long way to go to close the racial divide, but a large step was taken through the challenge of earthly authorities.

However, when doing so does not oppose our obedience to the kingdom of God, we are blessed by our submission to uninformed or even unjust authority structures. This positions us for God's blessing and leaves us in the position of allowing Him to be our defender and developer. King David realized this principle in how he dealt with the maniacal King Saul. Even though Saul treated him unjustly, David refused to retaliate, and God made up the difference.

Kingdom authority must flow in kingdom ways. This chapter highlighted some key principles for a consistent and ever-growing understanding and use of our authority as believers. The more we move in God's path, the more abundant the manifestation of His presence. So where do we go from here? We need to appropriate or take hold of our calling to be aligned with God. In the next chapter, I give some practical ideas on how to step into this calling.

CHAPTER SIX

"So What?" and "Now What?"

I f discussion of spiritual authority remains in the theologically abstract or in the narrative of past victories,
the purpose of this book is lost. I have written this
book about spiritual authority in response to people who
have heard me preach or teach around the world. When-
ever I talk about this provision for the Christian journey,
people ask me if I have written a book to explain more. My
experience is that everyone who has heard this teaching
and taken it to heart has seen radical changes in dealing
with the flesh, the world, and Satan. In saying this, I am
acknowledging once again that the journey of the Christ
follower is a struggle. If it were easy, we would not have
been offered the apostle's words at the end of his journey:
"I have fought the good fight. I have finished the race. I
have kept the faith" (2 Timothy 4:7). Nor would the writer
of the Epistle to the Hebrews have exhorted, "Let us throw
off everything that hinders and the sin that so easily en-
tangles, and let us run with perseverance the race marked
out for us" (Hebrews 12:1). So I now address the questions
of "So what?" and "Now what?" as practical responses on
how to move forward with our spiritual authority,

So What?

Knowing that the life journey is hard, why would we try to overcome spiritual opposition with limited resources? The opposition is stacked against us: We have the challenge of our own flesh that is bent against God, a world system that is moving away from God, and the enemy of our soul who leads a kingdom against our progress (Ephesians 2:1–3). Let's return to the earlier illustration of the traffic officer. We stand in the middle of the intersection, threatened by oncoming traffic—all more powerful than us. We will be run over if we do not raise our hands in authority and declare "The kingdom of God is here." In Christ we have been deputized to reign in the name of the king, and we carry the full force of the kingdom of God behind that declaration. We have already noted that the three most opposing forces are the flesh, the world, and Satan (Ephesians 2:1–3).

The battle begins against our own flesh—our sinful nature. Though in Christ we are declared spiritually new, we still are tied to the first Adam. Paul captures this inner struggle so graphically:

> I know that nothing good lives in me, that is, in my sinful nature (flesh). For I have the desire to do what is good, but I cannot carry it out. . . . No, the evil I do not want to do—this I keep doing. . . . It is sin living in me that does it. . . . But I see another law at work

in the members of my body, waging war against the
law of my mind and making me a prisoner of the
law of sin at work within my members.

(Romans 7:18–23)

Paul is desperate. His flesh is powerful and feels even
more powerful than his will. This is not the earlier, pre-dis-
ciple Saul speaking, as some commentators argue. This is
the fully alive Paul (Romans 6:1–14) who declares earlier in
the same letter, "I am not ashamed of the gospel, because it
is the power of God for the salvation of everyone who be-
lieves" (Romans 1:18). After professing his struggle he cries
out, "Who will rescue me from this body of death?" (1:24) In
words of praise he answers, **"Thanks be to God—through
Jesus Christ our Lord!"** Paul is not telling us to escape the
struggle by waiting for God to effect a change in us. We are
called to take an active role in our position in Jesus, and by
doing so, we take authority over our fleshly nature.

Daily in our journey, we also face the opposing winds of
worldly systems that are pushing against the advancement of
the kingdom. Embedded in these systems are strongholds, ar-
guments, and pretensions set against the knowledge of God.
Again Paul reminds us that we do not fight with weapons of
the world but, on the contrary, with weapons invested with
divine power to bring down those strongholds and places of
opposition (2 Corinthians 10:3–5). Paul uses warfare imagery
because of the combative nature of the struggle.

We can easily be lulled to sleep spiritually. Another author has described the active Christian life as attempting to climb to the next floor while on a downward moving escalator. In such a situation, we have to exert more energy just to keep in one place. We live in a world that is moving against the principles of God's kingdom. A passive stance still moves us away from our destination. How do we overcome this constant current against us? By our position of authority! We need to take an active stance.

Finally, there is a kingdom that actively opposes our success. Again the apostle reminds us that "our struggle is not against flesh and blood but against the rulers, against the authorities, against the powers of this dark world and against the spiritual forces of evil in the heavenly realm" (Ephesians 6:12). In the midst of this sober reminder, he exhorts us to stand, be strong, and put on the full armor. How? With authority! This is an active stance. The apostle James tells us to resist the devil and the devil will flee (James 4:7). Jesus himself noted that the church would need to be in advancement mode when he declared that "the gates of Hades would not prove strong enough" to resist the kingdom-invested followers of the Christ (Matthew 16:18–19). Gates may hold back, but they do not advance against the enemy. This imagery suggests that we are to be moving forward with authority to push back the kingdom of darkness.

Seated with Christ at the right hand of God—positioned with every rule and authority, power and dominion, squarely under our feet (Ephesians 1:20-22, 2:6)—we need to bring our flesh, this world, and the kingdom of darkness under God's reign. As C.S. Lewis noted in the introduction to Screwtape Letters, "Every moment and space is claimed by God and counterclaimed by Satan." I would add, "every person and territory," too. We are God's instruments to take back what belongs to Him. How is this possible when the powers are active and aligned against us? **Authority trumps power!**

What I want you to see at this moment is the need for a change in mindset. Most of us have been conditioned in a worldview of comfort. We are made to expect the faith journey to feel more like a cruise ship of luxurious comfort in the spiritual pursuit of happiness. Language of warfare is deemed archaic and politically incorrect, and makes us feel uncomfortable as followers of the Prince of Peace. In reality, we are nonetheless on a warship, in dangerous waters with an enemy launching torpedoes at us. We need to be on guard for our very lives and the lives of our loved ones around us.

I mean here our spiritual lives, which are easily marginalized in a world pushed deeper and deeper into a naturalistic and secular interpretation of reality that overemphasizes the material order and lifestyles of accumulation. Our spiritual lives are also diminished through philosophical underpinnings that make us blind to the spiritual activity, including warfare, that wages all around us. The result has been a spiritual sluggishness that leaves the inner person greatly underdeveloped. This reality often goes undetected until we face temporal crisis, even death, and we suddenly regret not having attended to the development of our spiritual side. Now is the time to take an active stance with our badge of authority.

Now What?

As followers of Christ, we have everything needed at our disposal. However, we must actively appropriate our authority, both in attitude and in action. In attitude means bringing all of our life into the experiential knowledge of this authority. We need to immerse ourselves in what it means to be positioned in Christ. (See Appendix 1.) We should study these verses until their profundity streams through the blood of our spiritual persons. We need to deepen our understanding of the kingdom of God. (See Appendix 2.) The gospel of the kingdom—the kingdom of God is here!—was Jesus's method and message. We need to weave this concept into our very worldview, knowing that when we hold up our hands of authority the full force of the kingdom is behind us.

All of this is about the "renewing of our minds" (Romans 12:2). One of the tactics of the enemy of our soul is false accusation; he is called the accuser of the brothers and sisters (Revelation 12:10). One of his lies encourages an attitude of acquiescence or surrender; Satan will whisper, "This is as good as it gets." God counters, "It only gets better as you are formed into an overcomer through this struggle." Another one of his lies is to caution people, "Be careful of this authority stuff. You're being presumptuous, and you'll probably abuse this authority." God responds, "Would I give you authority and then call you presumptuous for taking hold of it?"

When I allow God's Word to have greater hold in my mind and heart, then His truth shapes my response to the struggle of the journey. I do not passively accept; I actively announce. Again, this is not triumphalism. I will suffer. I will have challenges. But knowing that I am actively positioned in Christ, I can trust that those challenges are simply rocks in the stream of God's sovereign love and are part of the design to shape me into a victor. It is going back to original design—to rule, to reign, and to have dominion. All for the glory of the king!

This shift in attitude could be called "being." Sometimes it takes "doing" to create the habit of "being." It is a spiritual lifestyle. There are some actions that we can take to start embodying the lifestyle. The first is to actively appropriate our authority. I liken it to being dubbed a knight. Tim Keller has a great line in his book, The King's Cross: "We come before the king, bow the knee, lay our sword before him, and say 'Command me.'" I think it is wise to bow the knee before King Jesus and declare with open hands, "Here I am; I am positioned in you. I accept the mantle of your delegated authority. Now by your Spirit keep me vigilant and ready to take an active stance." Clearly the goal is to become an authority-wielding overcomer but it often begins with a declared decision.

I have found that where a fresh impartation of the Holy Spirit can come through the laying on of hands and prayer (which is consistent with Scripture), the authority of the believer is something that we need to take ahold of ourselves. Authority must be embraced. What does it mean to appropriate? It is to take hold of, to own, to actively engage. So maybe you should lay this book down at this moment and take hold of your calling and His provision. How? Simply bend the knee of your heart before the king of kings and pray something like this:

> I acknowledge you as king, my king. I do not have all of the *whys* and *hows* of this authority thing figured out. But I trust You and your Word. I willingly accept the mantle you have regiven me in Jesus, to join you in rule and reign, as I become an overcomer. By your Spirit, give me eyes to see when I am to be active in announcing your kingdom by actively taking spiritual authority. By your Spirit, help me to always use my authority within the principles of your design. And from this day forward, may all my prayers and acts of will be founded in the knowledge of my position of authority in Christ.

Once you have prayed this prayer, continue on with a new mindset and attitude of your deputation in Jesus Christ and live accordingly.

Other actions can help to declare our readiness for battle with this sense of authority. I have already mentioned the Lorica of St. Patrick (see Appendix 3 for the full prayer). I began praying the Lorica every morning for about four months. Then my wife and I rewrote it to read a bit more contemporary and added all of the aspects of the Christ event and some of the ways we have seen the kingdom of darkness oppose Christ followers. We memorized it, and we quote it every morning to start the day and then at different times throughout the day when it feels like we need a fresh stand. You will note the line that we added toward the end of the Lorica that clearly refers to our authority in Christ and our calling as gatekeepers:

> As I move into this day, I appropriate all this for myself and for all who are under my authority and influence.

Early in my spiritual journey, I found another exercise to be helpful in reinforcing a vigilant mindset and reminding me that I was not standing alone. Reciting Ephesians 6 (see the box below), I would stand in front of the mirror and gird myself with spiritual armor, actively appropriating every spiritual benefit invested in each piece. This action of

putting on armor took on new power as I became aware of
the authority behind the use of the armor. For some, this
might seem overdone. But I want to remind us that we have
lost a sense of the urgency of the battles that flare around
us. Remember, we have knelt before the king and are going forth in his battle orders. This sort of exercise (the em-
bodiment of what we believe) can solidify a newly learned
mindset or attitude. Today I will instinctively take up these
pieces of armor as I need them in battle.

I also find it helpful to picture or diagram the authority
structures of my life. Create a flow chart of your situational
authority structures. Who do you submit to? Observe the
past flow of authority into your life. Go back a couple generations in your family and in the organizations in which
you've been a member. You may realize that some of those
authority structures have not been rooted in Christ, and
you may need to reclaim a flow of Christ-centered authority. Over whom are you called to serve as a spiritual guardian? Then pray through your authority structure. Bless
those who have authority over you. Bless and protect those
who come under your authority and influence. I often pray
kingdom blessing to the third generation.

Finally, when you sense active opposition, experiment!
When your flesh rises up, don't just hold on and wait for it
to pass. Speak to your flesh authoritatively from your position of power. You are not victim. You are not captive. You
are overcomer. When the worldly systems push hard, com-

mand resistance. When the world tries to squeeze you into its way of thinking, take a stand with feet solidly planted, knowing that you do not stand alone. The kingdom behind you trumps all kingdoms of this world. When extraordinary, destructive obstacles challenge you, don't immediately assume that this is your assignment from God. Actively declare that you are seated with Christ, resist the devil, and open the gates of God's blessing on the situation. Speak healing with authority. Speak intervention with authority. Speak life abundance with authority. Speak protection with authority. Speak shalom-peace over your life, your household, your community—wherever God directs your attention—with authority.

Putting on the Spiritual Armor

Lord, you have instructed me by your Word to be strong in You and Your mighty power. You have commanded me to put on the full armor of God so that I can take my stand. I stand firm, then, with . . .

The Belt of Truth. The Belt of Truth pulls all of my pieces of armor together. The inner side of the Belt represents integrity. I want to live in congruency, where my outer person matches my inner person. Lord, as I put on the Belt of Truth, keep me honest and transparent in my relations with others, and keep my confession current with you. The outer side of the Belt represents discernment. Lord, as I buckle the Belt, give me spiritual eyes to see the opposition that stands against me so that I might take active authority against it.

The Breastplate of Righteousness. The breastplate covers all of my vital organs, most importantly my heart. Jesus is my righteousness. My attempts by my own strength at righteousness are like filthy rags compared to Your righteousness. Lord, as I put on the Breastplate of Righteousness, I am reminded that I am made acceptable to you through Jesus, and I ask you to live His righteousness through me by the Holy Spirit. Nothing can separate me from your love.

Feet Fitted with the Readiness of the Gospel of Peace. Being reconciled to God through Jesus Christ, I am called to be an ambassador of reconciliation in this world. Lord, as I put on the Gospel of Peace, I ask you to allow your light to shine through my life in order that people see you. And by your grace, may I be a peacemaker and not merely a peacekeeper.

Shield of Faith. I am increasingly aware that I have an enemy of my soul and that he opposes me. I take up the Shield of Faith to block his arrows. Faith is an active stance to believe your promises, Lord, instead of the lies of the enemy. At the core of your promises are two unchanging realities: you will never leave or forsake me, and greater is He who is in me than he who is in the world. Thus I am secure.

Helmet of Salvation. Boldness in the battle comes through right thinking. Two of the principal tools of the enemy of my soul are lies and accusation. In Jesus's name, I put on the Helmet of Salvation as I refuse the enemy's declaration about me. Lord, I choose rather Your declarations over me to shape my thought process. And I choose to fill my mind with things of life as opposed to things of death.

Sword of the Spirit. The Word of God is the Sword of the Spirit. This is the one offensive weapon of my armor. Lord, I take up your Word today to wield against the enemy of my soul. I ask you to illumine my mind by your Spirit so that I might understand it. I ask you to refresh my mind with the Word so that it is close at hand to use in battle. I ask you to give me courage to wield it through the actions of my life. Your Word will not return void or empty.

Lord, I trust in faith that as I have taken up each of these pieces of armor, you will activate their effectiveness throughout this day. Grant me discernment for when to actively employ each piece. And finally, I ask that you would pray prayers by your Spirit through me throughout this day. In Jesus's name, Amen.

I keep using the notion of speaking. You might be asking, "Do you really mean to verbalize a command opposing flesh, the world, or the kingdom of darkness?" Yes. If there is any potential that it is an assignment of the kingdom of darkness, it is in the declaration that authority is recognized. Even with the flesh? I believe that the kingdom of darkness knows our weaknesses and may put pressure in those places. So I do not spend much time in trying to decide which of the three areas might be active against me, I just command in my authority! The truth is that the flesh, the world, and the kingdom of darkness are not always easily separated. When I need to know the distinction, the Holy Spirit will provide discernment. Knowing that ultimately I am trusting the sovereign hand and direction of God, what is the worst thing that can happen in making a command? At the very least I simply reaffirm my position in Christ and in kingdom authority.

As I conclude this section, I want to offer an apology and an invitation. First, an apology. I believe that we, church leaders and communicators of God's Word, have failed the body of Christ by not emphasizing this truth from God's Word. We have left Christ followers unarmed and afflicted unnecessarily. I ask your forgiveness. Now calling for a fresh start of overcoming by the victory of the blood of Jesus, I offer this invitation. **Take your position and move out in authority.** I am setting up a webpage to collect your stories of taking up authority and the changes of circumstance that may have led from that. After you have experimented with wielding your Christ-given authority, I invite you to tell your story at www.authorityencounter.com to encourage others. What would happen if a critical mass of followers takes up spiritual authority in these days? Would it potentially lead to a strong advancement of the kingdom of light in this world?

> They triumphed over him by the blood of the Lamb
> and by the word of their testimony...
>
> (Revelation 12:11)

Postscript

Every person who has taken on the task of communicating God's Word does so with three clear realities. First, "there is nothing new under the sun" (Ecclesiastes 1:9), to use the words of the ancient preacher. We rediscover, repackage, and even re-explain with, hopefully, a fresh perspective or design. Many Christ followers have walked in spiritual authority in the past, and thus my insights are not new but may be presented in a fresh and concise manner. Second, there is no spiritual insight without the Holy Spirit, whether in retelling or in hearing. If there is any fruit in my teaching, and here in my writing, it is a result of the Holy Spirit bringing enlightenment to the process. I have been on a journey of discovery, to join a deep understanding of God's Word and Spirit-filled insight together in a practical theology. I did not intend to set out on this journey; I feel I have been guided by the Holy Spirit. Third, we stand on the shoulders of others who have gone before us. My knowledge of the impact of spiritual authority on daily life stems from a combination of insights and experiences from a number of people.

I was first introduced to the notion of spiritual authority by John MacMillan, who was a missionary in China and the Pacific Islands with the Christian and Missionary Alliance in the 1920s and 1930s. After the death of his wife, he returned to North America and landed as a professor at what is today Nyack College and Alliance Theological Seminary in Nyack, New York. Through practice as a businessman, missionary, pastoral minister, and professor, he learned to walk out his spiritual authority. He eventually had a series of journal articles published in a book entitled *The Authority of the Believer: A Compilation of "The Authority of the Believer" and "The Authority of the Intercessor."* As far as I can tell from my research, he was the first to systemize a practical theology of the authority of the believer into a comprehensive, book-length discussion.

I read an older edition of MacMillan's book from my grandfather's shelf in the late 1970s. I was captured by the analogy of the police officer, with which I prefaced this book. I later discovered that MacMillan borrowed this analogy from A.B. Simpson, the founder of the Christian and Missionary Alliance and Nyack Missionary Training Institute. I imagine that Simpson probably gleaned it from someone prior to his ministry. This exemplifies the "nothing new under the sun" principle—they were not creating new theology but reexpressing a long stream of practice of Christ followers throughout the ages. Simpson wrote in the *Alliance Weekly* on June 14, 1919, "...the policeman's badge which makes him mightier than a whole crowd of ruffians because, standing upon his rights, the power of the state is

behind him." Simpson went on to challenge Christ followers to use the authority of the name of Jesus to find victory
in the spiritual life. MacMillan took this illustration of the
police officer and made it a life teaching. He was my introduction to this concept of the authority of the believer as a
young theology student, and eventually as a young pastor
and missionary. Over the years, I have pursued this theology throughout Scripture and life experience. I have found
it to be biblically sound and experientially valuable. I am
grateful to be in the stream of this great biblical and Holy
Spirit tradition.

I was also influenced, or at least distantly instructed,
by a stream of practitioners from the academy. In the fall
of 1982, Fuller Theological Seminary offered a class, MC
510: "Signs, Wonders, and Church Growth." John Wimber
taught this class under the supervision of C. Peter Wagner.
Wagner and others from Fuller became distant mentors
for me as they began writing about their experiences. At
this time I began experiencing power evangelism and new
aspects of spiritual discipline such as prayer walking as a
pastor in New Jersey, and then as a missionary in France
and Mali, West Africa. Without an agenda or knowledge
of what others were doing, I would have completely new
experiences that made sense in light of my many years of
reading the Bible but that could not be categorized based
on knowledge gained through discipleship in the North
American church, in Bible training at a Christian liberal

arts college, or in evangelical seminary. Yet I would read an article from Wagner or a book from Wimber, and my experiences suddenly had biblical and theological handles. At the same time, Alliance Theological Seminary introduced a course called "Theology of Power Encounter." I returned to enroll in that week-long modular course and learned some principles to go along with what I was experiencing as I appropriated my authority in Christ.

Interestingly enough, in the early 2000s, I returned to Alliance Theological Seminary as a professor of Intercultural Studies, and I began teaching "Theology of Power Encounter." During this time, I used several books by Charles Kraft, also from Fuller, for classes that I taught. Kraft's book, *Behind Enemy Lines*, has been a constant on my syllabus for the power encounter class. Kraft has also written a book on the authority of the believer, *I Give You Authority* (which I did not use for the courses that I taught because I considered MacMillan's *The Authority of the Believer* a classic). I read Kraft's book on spiritual authority after completing my own writing of this book and realized in the reading how much I am in the flow of the Fuller stream and how much of Kraft's words have become part of my mindset. Even though I do not personally know the main players in the Fuller tradition, I feel a keen affinity in experience and practical theology. I feel like I stand on their shoulders. As a result of this history, I chose the title of this book intentionally.

In response to the Fuller movement, several professors and authors initiated an anti-charismatic reflex against the notions of Power Encounter. The American church in general had fully embraced the cultural notions of secularism, with its naturalistic explanations of daily phenomena. The church also developed a theology with an "excluded middle" (a concept originating with Charles Kraft, describing the dismissal by mainstream religious thought of the existence of spiritual beings other than God), while newcomers to America were reintroducing concepts of spiritual activity coming directly from spiritual powers other than God Almighty. Theologians found themselves in a rigid dichotomy—either evangelical (the Word) or charismatic (power). Oddly, many global theologians were trained in theological institutions that had been established by Westerners without a practical theology of dealing with spiritual power structures. I have run into this practical vacuum in many corners of the world. As I teach on spiritual authority in these contexts, believers are empowered with a new level of proactive resistance in the world in which they live.

This power vacuum among Bible-believing Christ followers created the space for a new teaching that tried to be a bridge between biblical and secular post-Enlightenment worldviews. The attempt to incorporate the world of Jesus and his immediate followers with the naturalized, contemporary world was well intentioned but still riddled with the fear of being perceived as archaic and lacking sophistication.

Most notable among those trying to bridge the two worldviews was Neil Anderson, who latched on to the notion of the "truth encounter" (*The Bondage Breaker*). Anderson's method was strongly rooted in an understanding that reintroduced Christ followers to their Christ-rooted position and authority to push back darkness in their own lives and around them. In his description, what was needed was a Truth Encounter—a change of mindset—not a Power Encounter. His intention was good and, I think, effective, even though he created a false dichotomy. Power Encounter and Truth Encounter are aspects of the same declaration in Jesus's name. When I read Anderson, I hear Power Encounter, even though he calls it Truth Encounter and says that power is not necessary. Truth is power.

I would suggest that Anderson was making an accommodation to the "excluded middle" of Western theologians and an overextended contextualization to American cultural values. The good that has come out of it is that many Christ followers have followed *The Bondage Breaker* method and found freedom as they have taken authority over the lies of Satan that have become part of their assumed reality. Anderson empowered believers to take a stand in their positional authority based on what God declares about us rather than what the enemy of our soul and our accuser whispers into our minds. The limitation in Anderson's perspective is that sometimes it takes more than changing our mindset; sometimes we need to resist forces outside of ourselves that are bringing more against us than wrong thinking.

I believe that the real bridge between power encounter and truth encounter is in the notion of **authority encounter**. Truth applied without authority is precept only—"knowledge without power." Power is always limited to who holds the most power at a given moment, but authority trumps power. We are all engaged in a daily Authority Encounter. The truth of God's Word and the enlightenment and power of the Holy Spirit become the guardrails to using this authority correctly, boldly, and without fear.

Finally, I am grateful to have had the opportunity to practice in pastoral ministry in New Jersey and Connecticut, in missionary ministry in France and Mali, in teaching ministry at Alliance Theological Seminary in New York, and in itinerant ministry in several countries around the world. In those places, I have had the opportunity to model and teach on this topic to the point that it has become an integral part of who I am as a person. In those multiple places, I have seen what happens when Christ followers take this position seriously. The transformation of your lives, and your encouragement to write the book, has kept the fire burning through the process.

I am grateful to each of those who play in the shaping of who I am today—in Christ, with authority, partnering with Him, to see the king glorified and the kingdom advance!

Now to him who is able to do immeasurably more than all we could ask or imagine, according to his power that is at work within us, to him be glory in the church and in Christ Jesus throughout all generations, for ever and ever! Amen.

Ephesians 3:20-21

Identity in Christ

P art of the process of walking in our authority is to establish in our minds a clear and bold understanding of our position in Christ. Our embraced identity shapes how we act out in this world. Right thinking will overcome feelings that speak against our identity, circumstances that seem to stand in the face of God's promises for us, and even the accusing voice of the enemy of our soul.

Being a Christ follower speaks to an inner transformation that has external ramifications. Being children of the light, we need to rehearse the statements of light spoken over us by God in His Word until they become our own patterns of thought. The old mystics referred to it as the Christ-life. As we take hold of this new identity in Christ, it will increase our sense of living out externally what we are already declared to be in Christ.

Some of us need the discipline of verbally rehearsing the following scriptural declarations until our heart actually owns them as truth. I find that verbal declaration is essential—it is the word of command. Some people may also find it helpful to make these declarations while looking into a mirror. I recommend doing this practice every day until these declarations become personal—and personalized—and not just for Christ followers in general.

I have heard people dismiss this as simply pop psychology. My response is that it is ancient theology. The apostle Paul, in Romans 12:2, writes,

> Do not conform any longer to the pattern of this world, but be transformed by the renewing of your mind. Then you will be able to test and approve what God's will is—his good, pleasing, and perfect will.

I encourage you to use the following truth statements from Scripture to reaffirm your identity in Christ, and then to live out that identity from the inside out.

Who I Am in Christ...

I Am Accepted

I am God's child.

John 1:12: *Yet to all who received him, to those who believed in his name, he gave the right to become children of God.*

I am Christ's friend.

John 15:15: *I no longer call you servants, because a servant does not know his master's business. Instead, I have called you friends, for everything that I learned from my Father I have made known to you.*

I have been justified.

Romans 5:1: *Therefore, since we have been justified through faith, we have peace with God through our Lord Jesus Christ.*

I am a son or daughter of God; God is spiritually my Father.

Romans 8:14–15: *Because those who are led by the Spirit of God are sons and daughters of God. For you did not receive a spirit that makes you a slave again to fear, but you received the Spirit of sonship and daughtership. And by him we cry, "Abba, Father."*

Galatians 4:6: *Because you are sons and daughters, God sent the Spirit of his Son into our hearts, the Spirit who calls out, "Abba, Father."*

I am a joint heir with Christ, sharing his inheritance with him.

Romans 8:17: *Now if we are children, then we are heirs — heirs of God and co-heirs with Christ, if indeed we share in his sufferings in order that we may also share in his glory.*

I am united with the Lord, and I am one spirit with Him.

1 Corinthians 6:17: *But he who unites himself with the Lord is one with Him in spirit.*

I have been bought with a price. I belong to God.
> 1 Corinthians 6:20: *You were bought at a price. Therefore, honor God with your body.*

I am a member of Christ's body.
> 1 Corinthians 12:27: *Now you are the body of Christ, and each one of you is a part of it.*

I am a saint.
> Ephesians 1:1: *Paul, an apostle of Christ Jesus by the will of God, to the saints in Ephesus, the faithful in Christ Jesus.*

I have been adopted as God's child.
> Ephesians 1:5: *He predestined us to be adopted as His sons through Jesus Christ, in accordance with His pleasure and will.*

I have direct access to God through the Holy Spirit.
> Ephesians 2:18: *For through him we both have access to the Father by one Spirit.*

I am a fellow citizen with the rest of God's family.
> Ephesians 2:19: *Consequently, you are no longer foreigners and aliens, but fellow citizens with God's people and members of God's household.*

I have been redeemed and forgiven of all my sins.
> Colossians 1:14: *In whom we have redemption, the forgiveness of sins.*

I am complete in Christ.

Colossians 2:10: *And you have been given fullness in Christ, who is the head over every power and authority.*

I am a son of light and not of darkness.

1 Thessalonians 5:5: *You are all sons of the light and sons of the day. We do not belong to the night or to the darkness.*

I am a child of God, and I will resemble Christ when he returns.

1 John 3:1–2: *How great is the love the Father has lavished on us, that we should be called children of God! And that is what we are! The reason the world does not know us is that it did not know Him. Dear friends, now we are children of God, and what we will be has not yet been made known. But we know that when He appears, we shall be like Him, for we shall see Him as He is.*

I Am Secure

I am a servant of righteousness.

Romans 6:18: *You have been set free from sin and have become slaves to righteousness.*

I am bound to God.

Romans 6:22: *But now that you have been set free from sin and have become slaves to God, the benefit you reap leads to holiness, and the result is eternal life.*

I am free from condemnation.

> Romans 8:1–2: *Therefore, there is now no condemnation for those who are in Christ Jesus, because through Christ Jesus the law of the Spirit of life set me free from the law of sin and death.*

> Romans 8:31–34: *What, then, shall we say in response to this? If God is for us, who can be against us? He who did not spare His own Son, but gave him up for us all—how will He not also, along with him, graciously give us all things? Who will bring any charge against those whom God has chosen? It is God who justifies. Who is he that condemns? Christ Jesus, who died—more than that, who was raised to life—is at the right hand of God and is also interceding for us.*

I am assured that all things work together for good.

> Romans 8:28: *And we know that in all things God works for the good of those who love Him, who have been called according to His purpose.*

I cannot be separated from the love of God.

> Romans 8:35–39: *Who shall separate us from the love of Christ? Shall trouble or hardship or persecution or famine or nakedness or danger or sword? As it is written: "For your sake we face death all day long; we are considered as sheep to be slaughtered." No, in all these things we are more than conquerors through him who loved us. For I am convinced that neither death nor life, neither angels nor demons, neither the present nor the future, nor any powers, neither*

height nor depth, nor anything else in all creation, will be able to separate us from the love of God that is in Christ Jesus our Lord.

I have been established, anointed, and sealed by God.

2 Corinthians 1:21–22: *Now it is God who makes both us and you stand firm in Christ. He anointed us, set His seal of ownership on us, and put His Spirit in our hearts as a deposit, guaranteeing what is to come.*

I am a new creation.

2 Corinthians 5:17: *Therefore, if anyone is in Christ, he is a new creation; the old has gone, the new has come!*

I am a prisoner of Christ.

Ephesians 3:1, 4:1: *For this reason I, Paul, the prisoner of Christ Jesus for the sake of you Gentiles . . . As a prisoner for the Lord, then, I urge you to live a life worthy of the calling you have received.*

I am confident that the good work God has begun in me will be perfected.

Philippians 1:6: *Being confident of this, that He who began a good work in you will carry it on to completion until the day of Christ Jesus.*

I am a citizen of heaven.

Philippians 3:20: *But our citizenship is in heaven. And we eagerly await a Savior from there, the Lord Jesus Christ.*

I am hidden with Christ in God.

Colossians 3:3: *For you died, and your life is now hidden with Christ in God.*

I am chosen of God, holy and dearly loved.

Colossians 3:12: *Therefore, as God's chosen people, holy and dearly loved, clothe yourselves with compassion, kindness, humility, gentleness and patience.*

1 Thessalonians 1:4: *For we know, brothers loved by God, that He has chosen you.*

I am a holy partaker of a heavenly calling.

Hebrews 3:1: *Therefore, holy brothers, who share in the heavenly calling, fix your thoughts on Jesus, the apostle and high priest whom we confess.*

I am a partaker of Christ; I share in his life.

Hebrews 3:14: *We have come to share in Christ if we hold firmly till the end the confidence we had at first.*

I can find grace and mercy in my time of need.

Hebrews 4:16: *It still remains that some will enter that rest, and those who formerly had the gospel preached to them did not go in, because of their disobedience.*

I am one of God's living stones, being built up in Christ as a spiritual house.

1 Peter 2:5: *You also, like living stones, are being built into*

a spiritual house to be a holy priesthood, offering spiritual sacrifices acceptable to God through Jesus Christ.

I am an alien and stranger to this world in which I temporarily live.

1 Peter 2:11: *Dear friends, I urge you, as aliens and strangers in the world, to abstain from sinful desires, which war against your soul.*

I am an enemy of the devil.

1 Peter 5:8: *Be self-controlled and alert. Your enemy the devil prowls around like a roaring lion looking for someone to devour.*

I am born of God, and the evil one cannot touch me.

1 John 5:18: *We know that anyone born of God does not continue to sin; the one who was born of God keeps him safe, and the evil one cannot harm him.*

I Am Significant

I am the salt of the earth and light of the world.

Matthew 5:13–14: *You are the salt of the earth. But if the salt loses its saltiness, how can it be made salty again? It is no longer good for anything, except to be thrown out and trampled by men. You are the light of the world. A city on a hill cannot be hidden.*

I am a branch of the true vine, a channel of His life.

John 15:1–5: *I am the true vine, and my Father is the gardener. . . . I am the vine; you are the branches. If a man remains in me and I in him, he will bear much fruit; apart from me you can do nothing.*

I have been chosen and appointed to bear fruit.

John 15:16: *You did not choose me, but I chose you and appointed you to go and bear fruit—fruit that will last. Then the Father will give you whatever you ask in my name.*

I am a personal witness of Christ.

Acts 1:8: *But you will receive power when the Holy Spirit comes on you; and you will be my witnesses in Jerusalem, and in all Judea and Samaria, and to the ends of the earth.*

I am God's coworker.

1 Corinthians 3:9: *For we are God's fellow workers; you are God's field, God's building.*

2 Corinthians 6:1: *As God's fellow workers we urge you not to receive God's grace in vain.*

I am God's temple—God's dwelling place. His Spirit and His life dwell in me.

1 Corinthians 3:16: *Don't you know that you yourselves are God's temple and that God's Spirit lives in you?*

1 Corinthians 6:19: *Do you not know that your body is a temple of the Holy Spirit, who is in you, whom you have received from God? You are not your own.*

I am reconciled to God and a minister of reconciliation for God.

2 Corinthians 5:17–21: *Therefore, if anyone is in Christ, he is a new creation; the old has gone, the new has come! All this is from God, who reconciled us to Himself through Christ and gave us the ministry of reconciliation: that God was reconciling the world to Himself in Christ, not counting men's sins against them. And He has committed to us the message of reconciliation. We are therefore Christ's ambassadors, as though God were making His appeal through us. We implore you on Christ's behalf: Be reconciled to God. God made him who had no sin to be sin for us, so that in him we might become the righteousness of God.*

I am seated with Christ in the heavenly realm.

Ephesians 2:6: *And God raised us up with Christ and seated us with him in the heavenly realms in Christ Jesus.*

I am God's workmanship, His handiwork, born anew in Christ to do His work.

Ephesians 2:10: *For we are God's workmanship, created in Christ Jesus to do good works, which God prepared in advance for us to do.*

I may approach God with freedom and confidence.

> Ephesians 3:12: *In him and through faith in him we may approach God with freedom and confidence.*

I am righteous and holy.

> Ephesians 4:24: *And to put on the new self, created to be like God in true righteousness and holiness.*

I can do all things though Christ who strengthens me.

> Philippians 4:13: *I can do everything through him who gives me strength.*

I am a member of a holy people, a people for God's own possession.

> 1 Peter 2:9–10: *But you are a chosen people, a royal priesthood, a holy nation, a people belonging to God, that you may declare the praises of Him who called you out of darkness into His wonderful light. Once you were not a people, but now you are the people of God; once you had not received mercy, but now you have received mercy.*

I am *not* the great "I am," but by the grace of God, I am what I am.

> Exodus 3:14: *God said to Moses, "I am who I am. This is what you are to say to the Israelites: 'I am has sent me to you.'"*

John 8:24: *I told you that you would die in your sins; if you do not believe that I am the one I claim to be, you will indeed die in your sins.*

John 8:28: *So Jesus said, "When you have lifted up the Son of Man, then you will know that I am the one I claim to be and that I do nothing on my own but speak just what the Father has taught me."*

John 8:58: *"I tell you the truth," Jesus answered, "before Abraham was born, I am!"*

1 Corinthians 15:10: *But by the grace of God I am what I am, and His grace to me was not without effect. No, I worked harder than all of them—yet not I, but the grace of God that was with me.*

Since I am in Christ, by the grace of God...

I have been justified—completely forgiven and made righteous.

Romans 5:1: *Therefore, since we have been justified through faith, we have peace with God through our Lord Jesus Christ.*

I died with Christ and died to the power of sin's rule over my life.

Romans 6:1–6: *What shall we say, then? Shall we go on sinning so that grace may increase? By no means! We died to sin; how can we live in it any longer? Or don't you know that all of us who were baptized into Christ Jesus were baptized into his death? We were therefore buried with him through baptism into death in order that, just as Christ was raised from the dead through the glory of the Father, we too may live a new life. If we have been united with him like this in his death, we will certainly also be united with him in his resurrection. For we know that our old self was crucified with him so that the body of sin might be done away with, that we should no longer be slaves to sin.*

I am free forever from condemnation.

Romans 8:1: *Therefore, there is now no condemnation for those who are in Christ Jesus.*

I have been placed into Christ by God's doing.

1 Corinthians 1:30: *It is because of Him that you are in Christ Jesus, who has become for us wisdom from God—that is, our righteousness, holiness, and redemption.*

I have received the Spirit of God into my life that I might know the things freely given to me by God.

1 Corinthians 2:12: *We have not received the spirit of the world but the Spirit who is from God, that we may understand what God has freely given us.*

I have been given the mind of Christ.

1 Corinthians 2:16: *"For who has known the mind of the*

Lord so as to instruct him?" But we have the mind of Christ.

I have been bought with a price; I am not my own; I belong to God.

1 Corinthians 6:19–20: *Do you not know that your body is a temple of the Holy Spirit, who is in you, whom you have received from God? You are not your own; you were bought at a price. Therefore, honor God with your body.*

I have been established, anointed, and sealed by God in Christ, and I have been given the Holy Spirit as a pledge guaranteeing our inheritance to come.

2 Corinthians 1:21–22: *Now it is God who makes both us and you stand firm in Christ. He anointed us, set His seal of ownership on us, and put His Spirit in our hearts as a deposit, guaranteeing what is to come.*

Ephesians 1:13–14: *And you also were included in Christ when you heard the word of truth, the gospel of your salvation. Having believed, you were marked in Him with a seal, the promised Holy Spirit, who is a deposit guaranteeing our inheritance until the redemption of those who are God's possession—to the praise of His glory.*

Since I have died, I no longer live for myself but for Christ.

2 Corinthians 5:14–15: *For Christ's love compels us, because we are convinced that one died for all, and therefore all died. And he died for all, that those who live should no longer*

live for themselves but for him who died for them and was raised again.

I have been made righteous.
2 Corinthians 5:21: *God made him who had no sin to be sin for us, so that in him we might become the righteousness of God.*

I have been crucified with Christ, and it is no longer I who live but Christ who lives in me. The life I am now living is Christ's life.
Galatians 2:20: *I have been crucified with Christ and I no longer live, but Christ lives in me. The life I live in the body, I live by faith in the Son of God, who loved me and gave himself for me.*

I have been blessed with every spiritual blessing.
Ephesians 1:3: *Praise be to the God and Father of our Lord Jesus Christ, who has blessed us in the heavenly realms with every spiritual blessing in Christ.*

I was chosen in Christ before the foundation of the world to be holy and am without blame before Him.
Ephesians 1:14: *Who is a deposit guaranteeing our inheritance until the redemption of those who are God's possession—to the praise of His glory.*

I was predestined—determined by God—to be adopted as God's son.

Ephesians 1:5: *He predestined us to be adopted as His sons through Jesus Christ, in accordance with his pleasure and will.*

I have been redeemed and forgiven, and I am a recipient of His lavish grace.
Ephesians 1:7–8: *In him we have redemption through his blood, the forgiveness of sins, in accordance with the riches of God's grace that He lavished on us with all wisdom and understanding.*

I have been made alive together with Christ.
Ephesians 2:5: *God . . . made us alive with Christ even when we were dead in transgressions — it is by grace you have been saved.*

I have been raised up and seated with Christ in heaven.
Ephesians 2:6: *And God raised us up with Christ and seated us with him in the heavenly realms in Christ Jesus.*

I have direct access to God through the Spirit.
Ephesians 2:18: *For through him we both have access to the Father by one Spirit.*

I may approach God with boldness, freedom, and confidence.
Ephesians 3:12: *In him and through faith in him we may approach God with freedom and confidence.*

I have been rescued from the domain of Satan's rule and transferred to the kingdom of Christ.

Colossians 1:13: *For he has rescued us from the dominion of darkness and brought us into the kingdom of the Son He loves.*

I have been redeemed and forgiven of all my sins. The debt against me has been canceled.

Colossians 1:14: *In whom we have redemption, the forgiveness of sins.*

Christ Himself is in me.

Colossians 1:27: *To them God has chosen to make known among the Gentiles the glorious riches of this mystery, which is Christ in you, the hope of glory.*

I am firmly rooted in Christ and am now being built in him.

Colossians 2:7: *Rooted and built up in him, strengthened in the faith as you were taught, and overflowing with thankfulness.*

I have been made complete in Christ.

Colossians 2:10: *And you have been given fullness in Christ, who is the head over every power and authority.*

I have been spiritually circumcised.

Colossians 2:11: *In him you were also circumcised, in the putting off of the sinful nature, not with a circumcision done by the hands of men but with the circumcision done by Christ.*

I have been buried, raised and made alive with Christ.

Colossians 2:12–13: *Having been buried with him in bap-*

tism and raised with him through your faith in the power of God, who raised him from the dead. When you were dead in your sins and in the uncircumcision of your sinful nature, God made you alive with Christ. He forgave us all our sins.

I died with Christ, and I have been raised up with Christ. My life is now hidden with Christ in God. Christ is now my life.

Colossians 3:1–4: *Since, then, you have been raised with Christ, set your hearts on things above, where Christ is seated at the right hand of God. Set your minds on things above, not on earthly things. For you died, and your life is now hidden with Christ in God. When Christ, who is your life, appears, then you also will appear with him in glory.*

I have been given a spirit of power, love, and self-discipline.

2 Timothy 1:7: *For God did not give us a spirit of timidity, but a spirit of power, of love, and of self-discipline.*

I have been saved and set apart according to God's doing.

2 Timothy 1:9: *Who has saved us and called us to a holy life—not because of anything we have done but because of His own purpose and grace. This grace was given us in Christ Jesus before the beginning of time.*

Titus 3:5: *He saved us, not because of righteous things we had done, but because of His mercy. He saved us through the washing of rebirth and renewal by the Holy Spirit.*

Because I am sanctified and am one with the Sanctifier, He is not ashamed to call me brother.

Hebrews 2:11: *Both the one who makes men holy and those who are made holy are of the same family. So Jesus is not ashamed to call them brothers.*

I have the right to come boldly before the throne God to find mercy and grace in time of need.

Hebrews 4:16: *Let us then approach the throne of grace with confidence, so that we may receive mercy and find grace to help us in our time of need.*

I have been given exceedingly great and precious promises by God by which I partake of God's divine nature

2 Peter 1:4: *Through these he has given us his very great and precious promises, so that through them you may participate in the divine nature and escape the corruption in the world caused by evil desires.*

The **Identity in Christ** declaration list has been circulating in various formats over the past few years. I have collected the statements from various sources. I recognize the later list, "Since I am in Christ…," as coming from the work of Neil Anderson. Neil has written an excellent book that reinforces the importance of taking our stand in life based on our identity in Christ, *Victory Over the Darkness: Realizing the Power of Your Identity in Christ.*

The Kingdom of God

Central to the message of Jesus was the idea of the kingdom of God. He announced at the beginning of his ministry, "The kingdom is at hand" (Mark 1:14–15, Luke 4:18–19, 43). Kingdom theology is important as a backdrop to an understanding of the significance of spiritual authority. This kingdom is referenced in multiple derivations in the New Testament: kingdom of God (52 times), kingdom of heaven (34 times), kingdom (10 times), kingdom of Christ, kingdom of the son of man, kingdom of His beloved son, and Jesus refers to it as "my kingdom" or "my Father's kingdom." Some writers have attempted complicated theologies from the use of different derivations of the name, but this is poor biblical scholarship. Each is referring to the same thing: God's rule.

When Jesus arrived on earth there was an expectation and hope for the invasion of God's rule over the kingdoms of this world. Thus, when Jesus spoke of the kingdom, many of his listeners were excited but held a different image than Jesus of what the kingdom would look like. Many people considered it as the day when God would come and restore His people, Israel as a unified geographical and political nation (John 6:15, Acts 1:6). Others saw it as the end of the present age, when God would create a new world in which evil, demons, sickness, and death would be defeated. However, Jesus had a more nuanced and spiritual view of the kingdom.

Jesus highlighted four aspects of the kingdom. First, it is a present spiritual reality (Mark 1:14–15) and thus seen in the demonstration or manifestation of God's way superimposed over the ways of this world. Second, it is a realm of authority in which His followers enter (Colossians 1:13) and then take with them (Luke 17:20-21). Third, it is very small and almost an unnoticeable force (Luke 13:18–21), like yeast that suddenly overtakes the whole dough. Finally, though, it is a kingdom that is experienced in the now; it is an inheritance that God will give fully to His people in the future (Matthew 25:34). It is the "now-and-not-yet" kingdom. In all of these descriptions is an air of mystery. The kingdom of God touches every aspect of our lives and yet is elusive due to its non-political and non-geographical reality.

In summary, the kingdom of God is the rule of God in my everyday life. As I submit to His ways, His rule comes to reign over my life and then through my life. I further participate in superimposing His rule over the broken structures of this world. An in-depth study of the kingdom of God would be valuable to better understand the notion of spiritual authority.

Aspects of the Kingdom

One Basic Demand: Repent (Mt. 3:2, 8 and 18:1–4)
One Essential Call: Seek (Mt. 6:33, Rom. 14:17)
One Comprehensive Identity: Servanthood
(Mk. 9:35, Mt. 20:25–28, Jn. 12:26)
One Never-Ending Resource: Holy Spirit (Jn.7:37–39)

The following Scriptures may be useful in developing a biblical theology of the kingdom.

(1) Nature of the kingdom of God

> Hebrews 12:28
> Colossians 1:13
> 1 Corinthians 4:20
> Romans 14:17
> John 18:36
> Luke 17:20, 21
> 2 Peter 1:11
> 1 Corinthians 15:50
> Luke 4:18, 19

(2) Membership in the kingdom of God

> Matthew 5:20

Matthew 7:21
John 3:3
John 3:5
Matthew 18:1–4
Mark 10:15
Mark 1:15

(3) The King of the kingdom

Hebrews 13:8
Revelation 17:14
Matthew 21:5
1 Timothy 1:17
Luke 1:31–33
Revelation 19:11–16
John 18:37

The following sources may be useful to develop further a theology of the kingdom of God.

John Bright, *The Kingdom of God*
George Eldon Ladd, *The Gospel of the Kingdom*
George Eldon Ladd, *New Testament Theology*
Allen Mitsuo Wakabayashi, *Kingdom Come*
Arthur F. Glasser, ed., *Announcing the Kingdom*

The Lorica of St. Patrick

The word *lorica* is actually a Latin word meaning "body armor." This prayer of Saint Patrick can be a means of the grace for you to be protected and shielded from all forms of ungodliness that arise from the devil and his demonic kingdom, the flesh, or the world.

I arise today
Through a mighty strength, the invocation of the Trinity,
Through a belief in the Threeness,
Through confession of the Oneness
Of the Creator of creation.

I arise today
Through the strength of Christ's birth and His baptism,
Through the strength of His crucifixion and His burial,
Through the strength of His descent for the
judgment of doom,
Through the strength of His resurrection and
His ascension,
Through the strength of the expectation and hope of
His imminent return.

I arise today
Through the strength of the love of cherubim,
In obedience of angels,
In service of archangels,
In the hope of resurrection to meet with reward,
In the prayers of patriarchs,
In preachings of the apostles,
In faiths of confessors,
In innocence of virgins,
In deeds of righteous saints.

I arise today
Through God's strength to pilot me,
God's might to uphold me,
God's wisdom to guide me,
God's eye to look before me,
God's ear to hear me,
God's word to speak for me,
God's hand to guard me,
God's way to lie before me,
God's shield to protect me,
God's hosts to save me,
From snares of the devil,
From temptations of vices,
From every one who desires me ill,
Afar and a-near, alone or in a multitude.

I summon today all these powers between me and evil
Against every cruel, merciless power that opposes my
body and soul,
Against all schemes and plans of the kingdom of darkness,
Against all curses and false judgments spoken
or unspoken,
Against all accusations and lies of the enemy,
Against all false agreements and unholy alliances,
conscious or unconscious,
Against every knowledge that corrupts man's
body and soul,
Christ shield me today!
Against any harm to my body, soul, or spirit,
Against any harm to my family, earthly or spiritual,
Against any harm to the earthly things you have called
me to steward,
So that I might live in the fullness of your blessing
and abundance.

Christ with me, Christ before me, Christ behind me,
Christ in me, Christ beneath me, Christ above me,
Christ on my right, Christ on my left,
Christ when I lie down, Christ when I sit down,
Christ when I arise,
Christ in the heart of every one who thinks of me,
Christ in the mouth of every one who speaks of me,
Christ in the eye that sees me,

Christ in the ear that hears me.

As I move into this day, I appropriate all this for myself and
for all who are under my authority and influence.

I arise today
Through a mighty strength, the invocation of the Trinity,
Through a belief in the Threeness,
Through confession of the Oneness,
Of the Creator of creation

St. Patrick (c. 377), Changes made by
Chuck and Ingrid Davis, 2012.

Bibliography

Anderson, Neil. 2000. *The Bondage Breaker*. Harvest House Publishers.

Clinton, Bobby. 1988. *The Making of a Leader*. Colorado Springs: NavPress.

Glasser, Arthur F. 2003. *Announcing the Kingdom: The Story of God's Mission in the Bible*. Grand Rapids, MI: Baker.

Kraft, Charles H. 1983. *Communication Theory for Christian Witness*. Nashville, TN: Abingdon Books.

Kraft, Charles. 1993. *Deep Wounds Deep Healing*. Ann Arbor, MI: Servant Publications.

Kraft, Charles. 1997. *I Give You Authority*. Grand Rapids, MI: Chosen Books.

Kraft, Charles H. with Mark White, ed. 1994. *Behind Enemy Lines*. Eugene, OR: Wipf and Stock Publishers.

Lewis, C.S. 1982. *The Screwtape Letters*. New York: Bantam Books.

MacMillan, John A. 1997. *The Authority of the Believer*. Camp Hill, PA: Christian Publications.

Wakabayashi, Allen Mitsuo. 2003. *Kingdom Come*. Downers Grove, IL: Inter-Varsity Press.

Scripture Index

ACKNOWLEDGMENTS

In the same way that I have come to my understanding of spiritual authority through the investment of many people in my life, the process of publishing those thoughts in a book is the result of many people. There are three who have been key in bringing the process to completion. Adrienne Daly, you have been such an asset as editor as you listened with me to discover my written voice. Thank you!

Megan Trank, you have been diligent, thorough, and accommodating in moving the raw material into a formatted book. Thank you!

Eric Kampmann, you have been the guide and motivation to help me arrive at my first published book. Beyond that professional role, you have been a friend of the Word with me, helping me tell the narrative of God's story in multiple, fresh ways. Thank you!

ABOUT THE AUTHOR

Chuck Davis is the Senior Pastor of Stanwich Church. He served seven years as Professor of Intercultural Studies at Alliance Theological Seminary. He earned his PhD in Sociology from Fordham University. Prior to his assignment as a professor, he spent ten years as a missionary in Mali, Africa. He has served actively in vocational ministry for over twenty-five years.